THOUSAND YEARS OF SPIRITUAL POETRY

The landscapes of the soul

— *Edited by Fiona Pagett* —

CHAUCER PRESS
LONDON

Published by Chaucer Press
an imprint of the Caxton Publishing Group
20 Bloomsbury Street
London WC1B 3JH

ISBN 1 904449 06 9

Designed and produced for Chaucer Press
by Savitri Books Ltd

ACKNOWLEDGEMENTS

'Rainbow' by **John Agard** from *Get Back Pimple*, published by Viking in 1996.
Reproduced by permission. 'Eden Rock' *from Collected Poems 1951-2000* by **Charles
Causley**, reprinted by permission of Macmillan and of David Higham Associates.
'Tenebrae' from *Poems of Paul Celan* by **Paul Celan**, translated by Michael
Hamburger, published by Anvil Press Poetry in 1988. Reprinted by permission of
the publisher and of Suhrkamp Verlag. 'Carpe Diem' by **Robert Frost** from *The
Poetry of Robert Frost, edited by Edward Connery Lathem*, the Estate of Robert Frost and
Jonathan Cape as publisher. Used by permission of The Random House Group
Limited. *The Poetry of Robert Frost, edited by Edward Connery Lathem* Copyright 1944
by Robert Frost, © 1969 by Henry Holt and Company. Reprinted by permission of
Henry Holt and Company, LLC. 'Prayer before Birth' from *Collected Poems* by **Louis
MacNeice**, published by Faber and Faber Ltd. Reprinted by permission of David
Higham Associates. 'Scorpion' by **Stevie Smith** from *Collected Poems of Stevie Smith*,
copyright © 1972 by Stevie Smith. Reprinted by permission of the Estate of James
MacGibbon and New Directions Publishing Corp. 'Last Poems' by **Rabindranath
Tagore** and 'On the Sick-Bed' from *Gitanjeli* and from *Collected Poems and Plays by
Rabindranath Tagore* reprinted by permission of Visva-Bharati, Santiniketan, India, on
behalf of the Estate of R.N. Tagore and New York: Macmillan, 1937). 'Kneeling' from
Collected Poems by **R.S. Thomas** reprinted by permission of the Publisher, JM Dent.
Poem by **Sri Vivekananda** from *The Gospel of Sri Ramakrishna*, as translated by
Swami Nikhilananda and published by the Ramakrishna-Vivekananda Center of
New York. Copyright © 1942 Swami Nikhilananda. Every effort has been made to
trace the copyright holders. The editor apologizes for any omission which may have
occurred.

CONTENTS

INTRODUCTION

Throughout the centuries, men and women of every culture have sought comfort in the face of the sorrows and uncertainties of their existence. By the same token, when things went well, they wanted to celebrate the joys of human or godly love, the beauty of nature and of life itself.

Poetry was, and still is, the ideal medium to record this quest for the spiritual, whether joyous, anxious or despairing. The oldest poem in this collection is four thousand years old, the most recent less than twenty. The authors come from as far afield as China and Guyana, and those who acknowledge a specific creed cover Christianity, Hinduism, Buddhism, Taoism and the ancient religions of Egypt and Greece. Their styles differ as widely as their content and tone, but all betray a great love of language and its capacity to recreate these 'landscapes of the soul'.

Some of the poems included here are overtly religious, from the confident passion for the god Krishna expressed by the Hindu mystic Mirabai to the anguish of Anne Brontë, who clearly found it difficult to believe that God took any notice of her at all. Others celebrate divine works – from the Vedic 'Song of Creation' to T. E. Brown rejoicing in God's gift of his simple garden in the Isle of Man and John Agard admiring the 'style' of the God who had the bright idea of creating the rainbow. Some seek to counsel those beset by the minor difficulties or major tragedies of life: Samuel Taylor Coleridge advises his reader to 'Ignore thyself, and strive to know thy God', while Ella Wheeler Wilcox cheerfully asserts 'Laugh, and the world laughs with you.' Yet others find that there is no comfort in this world and seek only the consolation of the next: Christina Rossetti sighs, 'If only I might love my God and die!', while Stevie Smith ends her poem 'Scorpion' with the despondent line, 'Scorpion so wishes to be gone.'

Strong faith has not always brought earthly happiness to its adherents, and a number of the writers included here suffered for their beliefs, or abandoned secular comforts in order to pursue spiritual ones. John Bunyan was imprisoned for twelve years for preaching without a licence; Fray Luis de Leon came into conflict with the Inquisition and spent four years in prison. Hildegard of Bingen was just one of those born to affluent circumstances who felt that chastity and obedience to the rule of her religious order were more important than a wealthy marriage. St Francis of Assisi went further and embraced poverty as well.

In England in the mid-seventeenth century, when religion was inseparable from politics, Milton's strong Puritan faith inevitably led him to espouse the Cromwellian cause – and equally inevitably to fall from grace following the Restoration of the monarchy. Two and a half centuries later, with worldwide communication becoming possible, Vivekananda was one of the first to preach spiritual understanding between east and west.

Many others of the writers in this collection contented themselves with preaching to their own parishes, or simply incorporated their faith into their daily lives. John Keats and Emily Brontë wrote moving poems when facing their own premature deaths. Louis MacNeice contemplates the world from the point of view of the unborn child, while E. Nesbit sees herself as a humble sinner, secure in the knowledge that God will forgive her, and the clergyman R. S. Thomas worries about his inadequacies as God's mouthpiece. Nor is this collection without its humour: Arthur Clough has his tongue firmly in his cheek when considering those who do or do not believe in God.

Whether expressing a closeness to God or to nature, conveying an awareness of the inner life or a preoccupation with the timeless dilemmas faced by human beings down the centuries and across cultures, the poems in this collection contain something that speaks to us all.

The most ancient sacred writings of the Hindus are the Vedas, *of which the* Rg Veda *forms part. It comprises over a thousand songs, compiled in about 2000* BC. *See also the much later* Bhagavadgita *(page 19).*

THE SONG OF CREATION

Then was not non-existent nor existent: there was no realm of air,
no sky beyond it.
What covered in, and where? and what gave shelter?
Was water there, unfathomed depth of water?

Death was not then, nor was there aught immortal: no sign was there,
the day's and night's divider.
That one thing, breathless, breathed by its own nature:
apart from it was nothing whatsoever.

Darkness there was: at first concealed in darkness, this All was
indiscriminated chaos.
All that existed then was void and formless: by the great power
of warmth was born that unit.

Thereafter rose desire in the beginning, Desire, the primal seed
and germ of spirit.
Sages who searched with their heart's thought discovered
the existent's kinship in the non-existent.

Transversely was their severing line extended: what was above it then,
and what below it?

There were begetters, there were mighty forces,
free action here and energy up yonder.

Who verily knows and who can here declare it, whence it was born
and whence comes this creation?
The gods are later than this world's production.
Who knows, then, whence it first came into being?

He, the first origin of this creation, whether he formed it all
or did not form it,
Whose eye controls this world in highest heaven, he verily knows it,
or perhaps he knows not.

The civilisation of ancient Egypt lasted roughly from the 27th to the 11th century
and throughout this period the people worshipped a pantheon of gods headed
by Osiris, king of the underworld, and his consort Isis. It is interesting to read
a poem from that period translated to suit a monotheistic audience.

GOD

is One and Alone,
and there is none other beside Him.
GOD is One and alone,
the Maker of all His creatures.
GOD is a Spirit,
deep-hidden from the eye of man and from all things.
GOD is the Spirit of spirits,

of creation the Spirit divine.

GOD is God from the beginning

before all things were He was God.

Lord of existences is He,

Father of all,

God external.

GOD is the One everlasting,

perpetual, eternal, unending.

From endless time hath He been,

and shall be henceforth and for ever.

GOD is hidden,

and no man His form hath perceived nor His likeness.

Unknown of gods and of men,

mysterious, incomprehensible.

GOD is Truth, and on truth doth He live;

King of truth divine is He.

GOD is life;

and man liveth through Him,

the Primeval Alone.

HOMER (c. 9TH CENTURY BC)

*Scholars have debated for centuries over the identity of the man who produced the great
Greek epics the* Iliad *and the* Odyssey. *Some put his dates as early as 1200 BC;
others insist that the two epics are not the work of the same man and that they were based
on ballads already in existence and adapted over a period of several hundred years.
Homer's birthplace is variously given as Smyrna, Rhodes, Colophon, Athens,
Salamis, Chios or Argos. Strangely, given this diversity of opinion,*

it is an accepted fact that he was blind.
This extract was translated by the poet Percy Bysshe Shelley.

Hymn to the Earth: Mother of All

O universal mother, who dost keep
From everlasting thy foundations deep,
Eldest of things, Great Earth, I sing of thee:
All shapes that have their dwelling in the sea,
All things that fly, or on the ground divine
Live, move, and there are nourished – these are thine;
These from thy wealth thou doth sustain; from thee
Fair babes are born, and fruits on every tree
Hang ripe and large, revered Divinity!

The life of mortal men beneath thy sway

Is held; thy power both gives and takes away!

Happy are they whom thy mild favours nourish,

All things unstinted round them grow and flourish.

For them, endures the life-sustaining field

Its load of harvest, and their cattle yield

Large increase, and their house with wealth is filled.

Such honoured dwell in cities fair and free,

The homes of lovely women, prosperously;

Their sons exult in youth's new budding gladness,

And their fresh daughters free from care or sadness,

With bloom-inwoven dance and happy song,

On the soft flowers the meadow-grass among,

Leap round them sporting – such delights by thee

Are given, rich Power, revered Divinity.

Mother of gods, thou wife of starry Heaven,

Farewell! be thou propitious, and be given

A happy life for this brief melody,

Nor thou nor other songs shall unremembered be.

LAO-TZU (c. 604 BC-?)

The name Lao-Tzu means 'old philosopher' and the man to whom this title is given is regarded as the founder of Taoism, which ranks alongside Buddhism and Confucianism as the principal religions of China. The Tao Te Ching *is the only record we have of Lao-Tzu's philosophy which, put in very simple terms, advocated a peaceful life lived in harmony with nature and with the universe.*

TAO TE CHING (EXTRACTS)

X

When carrying on your head your perplexed bodily soul
can you embrace in your arms the One
And not let go?
In concentrating your breath can you become as supple
As a babe?
Can you polish your mysterious mirror
And leave no blemish?
Can you love the people and govern the state
Without resorting to action?
When the gates of heaven open and shut
Are you capable of keeping to the role of the female?
When your discernment penetrates the four quarters
Are you capable of not knowing anything?
It gives them life and rears them.
It gives them life yet claims no possession;
It benefits them yet exacts no gratitude;
It is the steward yet exercises no authority.
Such is called the mysterious virtue.

XVI

I do my utmost to attain emptiness;
I hold firmly to stillness.
The myriad creatures all rise together
And I watch their return.
The teeming creatures
All return to their separate roots.
Returning to one's roots is known as stillness.

This is what is meant by returning to one's destiny.

Returning to one's destiny is known as the constant.

Knowledge of the constant is known as discernment.

Woe to him who wilfully innovates

While ignorant of the constant,

But should one act from knowledge of the constant

One's action will lead to impartiality,

Impartiality to kingliness,

Kingliness to heaven,

Heaven to the way.

The way to perpetuity.

And to the end of one's days one will meet with no danger.

The Therigatha *or 'Song of the Nuns', which dates from the 6th century* BC, *may be the earliest collection of women's writing in the world. The songs left by these early Buddhist nuns show how the teachings of the Buddha had liberated them from a life of drudgery or sorrow and enabled them to experience peace and inner freedom.*

A WOMAN WELL SET FREE! HOW FREE I AM

A woman well set free! How free I am,

How wonderfully free, from kitchen drudgery.

Free from the harsh grip of hunger,

And from empty cooking pots,

Free too of that unscrupulous man,

The weaver of sunshades.

Calm now, and serene I am,

All lust and hatred purged.
To the shade of the spreading trees I go
And contemplate my happiness.

THOUGH I AM WEAK AND TIRED NOW

Though I am weak and tired now,
And my youthful step long gone,
Leaning on this staff,
I climb the mountain peak.
My cloak cast off, my bowl overturned,
I sit here on this rock.
And over my spirit blows
The breath
Of liberty
I've won, I've won the triple gems.
The Buddha's way is mine.

The Bhagavadgita *is one of the principal sacred texts of Hinduism, written by members of the Bhagavata sect, probably some time between the 5th and 2nd centuries* BC. *These extracts were translated by the nineteenth-century English poet Sir Edwin Arnold.*

Yes! Thou art Parabrahm! The High Abode!
The Great Purification! Thou art God
Eternal, All-creating, Holy, First,
Without beginning! Lord of Lords and Gods!

Declared by all the Saints – by Narada,

Vyasa, Asita and Devalas:

And here Thyself declaring unto me!

What Thou hast said now know I to be truth,

O Kesava! that neither gods nor men

Nor demons comprehend Thy mystery

Made manifest, Divinest! Thou Thyself

Thyself alone dost know, Maker Supreme!

Master of all living! Lord of Gods!

King of the Universe! To Thee alone

Belongs to tell the heavenly excellence

Of those perfections wherewith Thou dost fill

These worlds of Thine: Pervading, Immanent!

How shall I learn, Supremest Mystery!

To know Thee, though I muse continually?

Under what form of Thine unnumbered forms

Mayst thou be grasped?

Ah! yet again recount,

Clear and complete, Thy great appearances,

The secrets of thy Majesty and Might,

Thou High Delight of Men! Never enough

Can mine ears drink the Amrit of such words!

SPIRITUAL POETRY

CAELIUS SEDULIUS (5TH CENTURY AD)

Sedulius's Carmen Paschale, *or* Easter Song, *from which this poem is an extract,
is regarded as the first Christian epic. An Irish bard who travelled to Rome,
Sedulius inspired Dante, Milton and others.*

INVOCATION

Eternal God omnipotent! The One
Sole Hope of worlds, Author and Guard alone
Of heaven and earth Thou art, whose high behest
Forbids the tempest's billow-bearing breast
The land to whelm – which fires the orb of noon,
And fills the crescent of the milder moon;
Who'st meted forth alternate day and night
And numbered all the stars – their places bright,
Their signs, times, courses only known to Thee –
Who hast to many forms, most wondrously,
The new earth shaped, and given to dead dust life:
Who hast lost Man restored, for fruit of strife
Forbid, bestown on him a higher food,
And healed the Serpent's sting by sacred blood:
Who hast, when men (save those borne in the Ark)
Were tombed in floods of whelming waters dark
From one sole stock again the race renewed
(A sign that sin-slain man, through noble wood
Once more should be redeemed), and sent to save
One Fount baptismal all the world to lave!
Open me the way that to the City bright

Leads forth; let thy Word's lamp be light

To guide my footsteps through the narrow gate,

Where the Good Shepherd feeds His sheep elate:

There first the Virgin's white Lamb entered

And all His fair flock followed where He led!

With Thee how smooth the way: for Nature all

Thine empire owns! Thou speak'st, her fetters fall

And all her wonted shows new forms assume:

The frozen fields will into verdure bloom

And winter gild with grain: if Thou but will

'Mid budding Spring the swelling grape shall fill,

And sudden labour tread the bursting vine.

All seasons answer to the call Divine!

So ancient Faith attests, so tell the hours –

No time can change, no age abate Thy powers!

Whereof to sing, in little part, afraid

I seek, as entering a great forest-glade

One strives an over-arching bough to reach.

What were an hundred tongues, an iron speech,

Or what were man an hundredfold to show

Things more than all the lucid stars that glow,

And all the sands where all the oceans flow!

ST PATRICK (c. 385-c. 461)

It is unlikely that Ireland's patron saint actually composed this verse, as scholars date it no earlier than the seventh century, but tradition has it that it acted as a breastplate of faith to protect the bodies and souls of Patrick and his followers against 'devils and men and vices'. The poem is therefore also known as St Patrick's Breastplate.

DEER'S CRY

I arise to-day
Through a mighty strength, the invocation of the Trinity,
Through belief in the threeness,
Through confession of the oneness
Of the Creator of Creation.
I arise to-day

Through the strength of Christ's birth with His baptism,
Through the strength of His crucifixion with His burial,
Through the strength of His resurrection with His ascension,
Through the strength of His descent for the Judgement of Doom.

I arise to-day
Through the strength of the love of Cherubim,
In obedience of angels,
In the service of archangels,
In hope of resurrection to meet with reward,
In prayers of Patriarchs,
In predictions of Prophets,
In preachings of Apostles,
In faiths of confessors,
In innocence of holy Virgins,
In deeds of righteous men.

I arise to-day
Through the strength of heaven,
Light of sun,
Radiance of moon,
Splendour of fire,
Speed of lightning,
Swiftness of wind,
Depth of sea,
Stability of earth,
Firmness of rock.

I arise to-day
Through God's strength to pilot me,

God's might to uphold me,
God's wisdom to guide me,
God's eye to look before me
God's ear to hear me,
God's word to speak for me,
God's hand to guard me,
God's way to lie before me,
God's shield to protect me,
God's host to save me
From snares of devils,
From temptations of vices,
From every one who shall wish me ill,
Afar and anear,
Alone and in a multitude.

I summon to-day all these powers between me and those evils,
Against every cruel merciless power that may oppose my body and my soul,
Against incantations of false prophets,
Against black laws of pagandom,
Against false laws of heretics,
Against craft of idolatry,
Against spells of women and smiths and wizards,
Against every knowledge that corrupts man's body and soul.

Christ to shield me to-day
Against poison, against burning,
Against drowning, against wounding,
So that there may come to me abundance of reward.
Christ with me, Christ before me, Christ behind me,
Christ in me, Christ beneath me, Christ above me,

Christ on my right, Christ on my left,

Christ when I lie down, Christ when I sit down, Christ when I arise,

Christ in the heart of every man who thinks of me,

Christ in the mouth of every one who speaks of me,

Christ in every eye that sees me,

Christ in every ear that hears me.

I arise to-day

Through a mighty strength, the invocation of the Trinity,

Through belief in the threeness,

Through confession of the oneness

Of the Creator of Creation.

The following two anonymous poems, both Irish and dating from the tenth century, show the ambivalent attitude to women – the purity of the Virgin Mary contrasted with the blame accorded to Eve for the Fall of Man – which prevailed throughout the Catholic Church in the medieval period.

EVE'S LAMENT

I am Eve, great Adam's wife,

'Tis I that outraged Jesus of old;

'Tis I that robbed my children of Heaven,

By right 'tis I that should have gone upon the cross.

I had a kingly house to please me,

Grievous the evil choice that disgraced me,

Grievous the wicked advice that withered me!
Alas! my hand is not pure.

'Tis I that plucked the apple,
Which went across my gullet:
So long as they endure in the light of day,
So long women will not cease from folly.

There would be no ice in any place,
There would be no glistening windy winter,
There would be no hell, there would be no sorrow,
There would be no fear, if it were not for me.

PRAYER TO THE VIRGIN

Gentle Mary, noble maiden, give us help!
Shrine of our Lord's body, casket of the mysteries!

Queen of queens, pure holy maiden,
Pray for us that our wretched transgression be forgiven for thy sake.

Merciful one, forgiving one, with the grace of the Holy Spirit,
Pray with us to the true-judging King of the goodly ambrosial clan.

Branch of Jesse's tree in the beauteous hazel-wood,
Pray for me until I obtain forgiveness of my foul sins.

Mary, splendid diadem, thou that hast saved our race,
Glorious noble torch, orchard of Kings!

Brilliant one, transplendent one, with the deed of pure chastity,
Fair golden illumined ark, holy daughter from Heaven!

Ladder of the great track by which every saint ascends,
Mayst thou be our safeguard towards the glorious Kingdom.

Fair fragrant seat chosen by the King,
The noble guest who was in thy womb three times three months.

Glorious royal porch through which He was incarnated,
The splendid chosen sun, Jesus, Son of the living God.

For the sake of the fair babe that was conceived in thy womb,
For the sake of the holy child that is High-King in every place,

For the sake of His cross that is higher than any cross,
For the sake of His burial when He was buried in a stone-tomb,

For the sake of His resurrection when He arose before every one,
For the sake of the holy household from every place to Doom,

Be thou our safeguard in the Kingdom of the good Lord,
That we may meet with dear Jesus – that is our prayer – hail!

Mother of righteousness, Thou that excellest all else,
Pray with me thy first-born to save me on the day of Doom.

Noble rare star, tree under blossom,
Powerful choice lamp, sun that warmeth every one.

SPIRITUAL POETRY

HILDEGARD OF BINGEN (1089-1179)

Although her origins were noble and she could doubtless have married well and lived in luxury, Hildegard of Bingen spent most of her long life at the convent of Disibodenberg in the Rhineland, where she became abbess in 1136. Most unusually for a woman of her time, she travelled throughout Germany to preach and became known as a mystic and prophet. Her early mystical writings were inspired by visions (cf Teresa of Avila, page 43) and are often compared to the works of Dante and Blake. Later in life she wrote a number of religious songs which are still widely sung and recorded today.

SYMPHONY OF THE HARMONY OF CELESTIAL REVELATIONS (EXTRACTS)

Hail, Mary, author of life,
you have rebuilt our salvation.

You have shaken death

and destroyed the serpent

to which Eve rose up

with head held high in the breath of her pride.

You trampled it down

when you gave birth to the Son of God from heaven.

By the inspiration of the Spirit of God.

Sweet and loving Mother, we greet you,

You have granted the world your child sent from heaven,

By the inspiration of the Spirit of God.

Glory be to the Father and to the Son and to the Holy Spirit,

By the inspiration of the Spirit of God.

ʾ◆ʾ◆

O bright Mother of holy medicine

You have poured out the ointment, through your holy Son,

on the grieving wounds of death

which Eve originated to the torment of souls.

You have destroyed death

which Eve originated to the torment of souls.

You have destroyed death

and built up life.

Pray for us to your Son,

O Mary, Star of the Sea.

O giver of life and splendour of joys

O sweetness of all delights, in you never fading!

Pray for us to your Son,

O Mary, Star of the Sea.

Glory be to the Father and to the Son and to the Holy Spirit.

Pray for us to your Son,

O Mary, Star of the Sea.

༺▲༻

Most splendid of gemstones!

Bright beauty of the sun!

He poured upon you,

as a leaping fountain from the heart of the Father,

His unique and only Word,

through whom he made the primal matter of the world

which Eve the woman threw into confusion.

In your image, Father, this Word created the human being.

Therefore, Mary, you are the bright matter

through which the Word breathed all the virtues forth,

as once he led forth, in the primal matter of the world, the whole of creation.

FARID AD-DIN ATTAR (?1142-?1207)

Born in Nishapur in what was then Persia, Attar is among the foremost poets of the mystical Islamic sect known as Sufi. His greatest work is The Parliament of the Birds, *an allegory of the soul's search for divine truth. It was translated by Edward Fitzgerald, better known for his version of* The Rubáiyát of Omar Khayyám.

THE PARLIAMENT OF THE BIRDS (EXTRACT)

Once more they ventured from the dust to raise

Their eyes – up to the throne – into the blaze,

And in the centre of the Glory there
Beheld the figure of – themselves – as 'twere
Transfigured – looking to themselves, beheld
The figure on the throne en-miracled,
Until their eyes themselves and *that* between
Did hesitate which *seer* was, which *seen*;
They That, That They: another, yet the same;
Dividual, yet one: from whom there came
a voice of awful answer, scarce discern'd,
From *which* to aspiration, *whose* return'd
They scarcely knew; as when some man apart
Answers aloud the question in his heart:
The sun of my perfection is a glass
Wherein from *seeing* into *being* pass.

IMMERSE YOURSELF FOR EVERMORE

Meditate, O my mind, on the Lord,
The Stainless One, Pure Spirit through and through.
How peerless is the light that in Him shines!
How soul-bewitching is His wondrous form!
How dear is He to all His devotees!

Ever more beauteous in fresh-blossoming love
That shames the splendour of a million moons,
Like lightning gleams the glory of His form,
Raising erect the hair for very joy.

Worship His feet in the lotus of your heart;
With mind serene and eyes made radiant

With heavenly love, behold that matchless sight.
Caught in the spell of His love's ecstasy,
Immerse yourself for evermore, O mind,
In Him who is Pure Knowledge and Pure Bliss.

ST FRANCIS OF ASSISI (1181-1226)

Born into a prosperous merchant's family, St Francis led a fun-loving and extravagant life until he reached his early twenties, when a serious illness followed by a vision persuaded him to devote himself to the care of the poor and sick. He founded the Franciscan order of monks, committed to poverty, chastity and obedience, but particularly to poverty – he lived as a hermit and gave up all his possessions. His hymns, remarkable for their simplicity, were among the first written in Italian rather than Latin.

A PRAYER

Lord, make me an instrument of Thy Peace.
Where there is hatred, let me sow love;
Where there is injury, pardon;
Where there is doubt, faith;
Where there is despair, hope;
Where there is darkness, light;
Where there is sadness, joy.

O Divine Master, grant that I may not so much seek to be consoled as to console;
to be understood, as to understand;
to be loved, as to love.
For it is in giving that we receive;

It is in pardoning that we are pardoned;
It is in dying that we are born to eternal life.

KABIR (BORN ?1455)

Biographical information about the fifteenth-century Indian weaver-sage is scanty. He belonged to the weaver caste but it is uncertain whether he was born a Hindu or a Muslim. In childhood he became a disciple of one of the leading Hindu sages of his time, but throughout his life described himself as being neither a Hindu nor a Muslim, but 'an ensemble of five elements in which the spirit plays its drama of joy and suffering'. HIs writings advocate tolerance and understanding among all peoples, and preach that Divine love is near at hand for anyone who takes the trouble to look and to experience. He left thousands of songs and couplets which are still sung and recited today and he had a unique influence on the development of northern Indian literature.

IN PRAISE OF THE GURU (EXTRACTS)

I

My teacher and my Master
Both stand here
Before me.
To whom
Shall I bow first?

O seeker,
Hail thy teacher!
It is he
Who has made

This union
With the Master
Possible.

II

The guru
Is a potter
And the pupil
A pot.

How it hurts
When he thumps
From the outside,
But see
How delicately
He supports
From the inside,
So a beautiful pot
May be created.

III

Like moths
Hovering
Over the flame,
We burn ourselves
To ashes
In illusion!
O Kabir
It is only
A rare man
Who escapes

This destruction
With the guidance
Of the guru.

VI
A shower
Of pearls
Has poured over
The earth,
How the seekers
Yearn to
Collect them!
Those who have the guidance
Of a guru,
Gather many.
The others are left
Empty-handed.

VIII

If the guru himself

Be blind,

How can the pupil

Hope to see

The light?

O seeker

When the blind

Lead the blind,

Both fall

Into a ditch!

X

O friend

All seekers know

The distinction

Between the philosopher's stone

And the guru:

One changes base metals

Into gold

And the other

Transforms the man himself!

ONE, ONLY ONE

I

Wherever

My eyes turn

I see
His illumination.

O my friends
When I reach out
To touch it,
I too
Become part
Of the illumination.

IV

I have searched
For Him
Everywhere,
But to no avail.

O friend, listen.
He and I are One.

When the ocean
Is submerged
In the drop,
Who can say
What is what?

VIII

Ice is only
Frozen water,
With the heat
Of the sun

It turns into
Water again.

What a joy, O Kabir
To return
To the source!
What was
Is
There is nothing more
To be said.

Sand and stone
They have piled,
And they call it
A mosque!

And there
How like a hawker
The priest shouts
The name of Allah,
As though
God were deaf!

Look at these men,
O Kabir
How their god
Is on sale,
And how in blind pursuit
And sheer imitation
Of one another,

They go to places
Of pilgrimage
Performing
Empty rituals.

Lost and bewildered!

MIRABAI (c. 1498-1565)

Born into a powerful and wealthy family and married to a Rajput crown prince, Mirabai
abandoned the lavish gifts given to her on her wedding day and devoted her adult life to
the worship of the god Giridhar Naagar, an aspect of Krishna, whom she regarded as her

real husband. The ecstasy with which she describes their relationship has an earthly, sexual quality which makes an interesting comparison with the writings of her near-contemporary St Teresa of Avila (see page 43).

I AM PALE WITH LONGING FOR MY BELOVED

I am pale with longing for my beloved;
People believe I am ill.
Seizing on every possible pretext,
I try to meet him 'by accident'.

They have sent for a country doctor;
He grabs my arm and prods it;
How can he diagnose my pain?
It's in my heart that I am afflicted.

Go home, country doctor,
Don't address me by my name;
It's the name of God that has wounded me,
Don't force your medicines on me.

The sweetness of his lips is a pot of nectar,
That's the only curd for which I crave;
Mira's Lord is Giridhar Naagar.
He will feed me nectar again and again.

SPIRITUAL POETRY

I Am True to my Lord

I am true to my Lord.
O my companions, there is nothing to be ashamed of now
Since I have been seen dancing openly.

In the day I have no hunger
At night I am restless and cannot sleep.
Leaving these troubles behind, I go to the other side;
A hidden knowledge has taken hold of me.

My relations surround me like bees.
But Mira is the servant of her beloved Giridhar,
And she cares nothing that people mock her.

St Teresa of Avila (1515-1582)

Teresa of Avila, who was canonised in 1622, spent most of her life in a
Carmelite convent, but like Hildegard of Bingen travelled in the cause of God,
founding convents and reforming the Carmelite order. Her mystical visions inspired her
writings, which convey her yearning to be the bride of Christ. Like Mirabai (above) and
Emily Dickinson four centuries later (see page 119), she often used the language of
romantic or earthly passion to express her love of God.

My Beloved One Is Mine

I gave myself to Love Divine,
And lo! my lot so changed is

That my Beloved One is mine

And I at last am surely His.

When that sweet Huntsman from above

First wounded me and left me prone,

Into the very arms of Love

My stricken soul forthwith was thrown.

Since then my life's no more my own

And all my lot so changed is

That my Beloved One is mine

And I at last am surely His.

FRAY LUIS DE LEON (?1527-1591)

Written in a simple style that forms a sharp contrast to the extravagant verse of his contemporaries, Fray Luis's work examines the distinction between the day-to-day concerns of mankind and what he saw as the reality of spiritual life. His views brought him into conflict with the Inquisition, as a result of which he spent four years in prison.

A RETIRED LIFE

What a restful life is his

Who flees the noisy world

And follows the hidden path

Down which have travelled

The few wise men the world has known!

For his heart is not troubled

By the state of the proud and the great

Nor does he marvel at the roof
Built by the skilful Moor
Adorned with gold and supported by columns of jasper.

It does not bother him
Whether fame sings his praises
Or extols with a flattering tongue
That which honest truth condemns.

If vain fingers point me out,
Does it add to my happiness?
If I chase after fame,
Do I not arrive breathless,
With anxious longings and mortal cares?

Oh mountain! oh spring! oh river!
Oh safe and delightful hiding place!
With my ship almost wrecked
I flee from the stormy seas
To your restful calm.

I ask only for peaceful sleep
And pure, cheerful, free days;
I don't want to be frowned upon
By one who cares only for birth or money.

I want to wake up to the sound of birds
Singing their delicious and untaught song,
Not to the heavy cares which pursue
A man who is subject to the will of another.

SPIRITUAL POETRY

I want to live alone,
To enjoy, in solitude and without witnesses,
Only the wealth that I owe to heaven,
Free from love and jealousy,
From hatred, hopes and suspicions.

On the mountainside I have a garden
Planted by my own hand
Which in spring is covered
With beautiful flowers
And shows the certain hope of fruit.

And as if eager to see it
And increase its beauty,
A pure spring races
From the proud mountain-top,
Hurrying to reach it.

And there, tranquilly,
Twisting its way among the trees
And clothing in green
The ground it passes through
It scatters a variety of flowers.

The soft wind fans the garden
And offers up a thousand scents to the senses.
It sways the trees with a gentle sound
Which casts gold and sceptres into oblivion.

Let those who trust themselves
To a weak ship, have their treasure.

I do not have to see the weeping
Of those who despair
When the north and south winds blow too fiercely.

The mast creaks under the onslaught
And bright day turns to blind night;
A confused clamour sounds up to the heavens,
As these men cast their riches into the sea.

Let a poor little table,
Well stocked with beloved peace, suffice for me,
And let the plate shaped from fine gold
Go to him who does not fear
The sea when it is angry.

And while those others burn in misery
With an insatiable thirst
For a power which will not last
Let me be stretched out in the shade,
Singing.

Stretched out in the shade,
Crowned with ivy and everlasting laurel,
With my ear listening attentively
To the measured sound
Of a skilfully plucked plectrum.

❧

SPIRITUAL POETRY

❧❧❧

SIR WALTER RALEIGH (?1554-1618)

Queen Elizabeth I's favoured courtier and explorer fell from grace under James I –
he spent most of the last fifteen years of his life imprisoned in the Tower of London
on a charge of high treason and was eventually executed. During his time
in prison he embarked on an ambitious project to write the History of the World
but completed only one volume; its 1300 pages cover Egyptian, Greek
and Roman history to the second century BC, *although the Preface shows*
that he intended to continue up to his own times. Some doubt surrounds
the authenticity of a number of poems once attributed to Raleigh, although
he is known to have written an epitaph to his friend Sir Philip Sidney,
and a prefatory sonnet to Edmund Spenser's epic Faerie Queene.
This poem was probably written in the Tower.

What Is our Life?

What is our life? A play of passion,
And what our mirth but music of division?
Our mothers' wombs the tiring-houses be
Where we are drest for this short comedy,
Heaven the judicious sharp spectator is
Who sits and marks what here we do amiss.
The graves that hide us from the searching sun
Are like drawn curtains when the play is done.
Thus playing post we to our latest rest,
And then we die, in earnest, not in jest.

Sir Philip Sidney (1554-1586)

Soldier, diplomat, writer and patron of the arts, Philip Sidney embodies the ideal of 'Renaissance man'. He was both well connected and generous, a fact which might have contributed to the great popularity of his writing during his lifetime. However, the merit of his work has stood the test of time and it seems likely that, had he not died in battle at such a young age, he would have gone on to write poetry to rival that of his more famous contemporaries.

Why Fear to Die?

Since Nature's works be good, and death doth serve
As Nature's work, why should we fear to die?
Since fear is vain but when it may preserve,
Why should we fear that which we cannot fly?

Fear is more pain than is the pain it fears,

Disarming human minds of native might;

While each conceit an ugly figure bears,

Which were not evil, well view'd in reason's light

Our only eyes, which dimm'd with passions be,

And scarce discern the dawn of coming day,

Let them be clear'd, and now begin to see

Our life is but a step in dusty way:

Then let us hold the bliss of peaceful mind,

Since this we feel, great loss we cannot find.

WILLIAM SHAKESPEARE (1564-1616)

Most of Shakespeare's 150 sonnets are undisputedly concerned with earthly love, but this one reveals a more spiritual side. In addition to writing sonnets and a number of longer poems, he frequently incorporated songs and verses into his plays, some of them of a sombre and brooding nature.

SONNET 146

Poor soul, the centre of my sinful earth,

Fooled by these rebel powers that thee array,

Why dost thou pine within and suffer dearth,

Painting thy outward walls so costly gay?

Why so large cost, having so short a lease,

Dost thou upon thy fading mansion spend?

Shall worms, inheritors of this excess,

Eat up thy charge? Is this thy body's end?

Then, soul, live thou upon thy servant's loss,
And let that pine to aggravate thy store;
Buy terms divine in selling hours of dross;
Within be fed, without be rich no more;
So shalt thou feed on Death, that feeds on men,
And Death once dead, there's no more dying then.

FIDELE (from *Cymbeline*)

Fear no more the heat o' the sun,
Nor the furious winter's rages;
Thou thy worldly task has done,
Home art gone, and ta'en thy wages.
Golden lads and girls all must,
As chimney-sweepers, come to dust.

Fear no more the frown o' the great,
Thou are past the tyrant's stroke;
Care no more to clothe and eat;
To thee the reed is as the oak:
The sceptre, learning, physic, must
All follow this, and come to dust.

Fear no more the lighting-flash,
Nor the all-dreaded thunder-stone;
Fear not slander, censure rash;
Thou hast finish'd joy and moan:
All lovers young, all lovers must
Consign to thee and come to dust.

SPIRITUAL POETRY

No exorciser harm thee!

Nor no witchcraft charm thee!

Ghost unlaid forbear thee!

Nothing ill come near thee!

Quiet consummation have;

And renownèd be thy grave!

WILLIAM ALABASTER (1568-1640)

William Alabaster had a varied career that included a period as chaplain to the
Protestant Queen Elizabeth's favourite the Earl of Essex, whom he accompanied
on his successful expedition to sack Cadiz in 1596. Alabaster's subsequent
conversion to Catholicism resulted in his being arrested and removed from
holy orders. Some years later, his first essay in mystical theology was declared heretical,

an event which led to his leaving his adopted church and reverted to Protestantism. Alabaster's early work included highly regarded Latin verse; this was followed by a collection of sonnets in English, mostly on a metaphysical or devotional theme.

TO BE BORN IS GOD'S GREATEST GIFT

Like as the fountain of all light created
Doth pour out streams of brightness undefined
Through all the conduits of transparent kind,
That heaven and air are both illuminated,
And yet his light is not thereby abated;
So God's eternal bounty ever shined
The beams of being, moving, life, sense, mind.
And to all things himself communicated
But for the violent diffusive pleasure
Of goodness, that left not till God had spent
Himself, by giving us himself his treasure
In making man a God omnipotent.
How might this goodness draw ourselves above
Which drew down God with such attractive love!

JOHN DONNE (1573-1631)

Although born a Catholic (which prevented him taking a degree at Oxford or Cambridge, both of which he attended while in his teens), Donne seems to have abandoned this faith by the time he was twenty. After a lengthy period of disgrace and poverty following an imprudent marriage, he finally entered the Anglican church in 1615. Much of Donne's early work is satirical and erotic. His later devotional work retains the same passion, though his fervour is now directed towards the divine.

HOLY SONNETS (EXTRACTS)

X

Death, be not proud, though some have callèd thee
Mighty and dreadful, for thou art not so:
For those whom thou think'st thou dost overthrow
Die not, poor Death; nor yet canst thou kill me.
From Rest and Sleep, which but thy picture be,
Much pleasure, then from thee much more must flow;
And soonest our best men with thee do go –
Rest of their bones and souls' delivery!
Thou'rt slave to fate, chance, kings, and desperate men,
And dost with poison, war, and sickness dwell;
And poppy or charms can make us sleep as well
And better than thy stroke. Why swell'st thou then?
One short sleep past, we wake eternally,
And Death shall be no more: Death, thou shalt die!

XIV

Batter my heart, three person'd God; for you
As yet but knock, breathe, shine and seek to mend;
That I may rise, and stand, o'erthrow me, and bend
Your force, to break, blow, burn and make me new.

I, like an usurpt town, to'another due,

Labour to admit you, but Oh, to no end,

Reason your viceroy in me, me should defend,

But is captiv'd, and proves weak or untrue,

Yet dearly I love you, and would be lov'd fain

But am betroth'd unto your enemy,

Divorce me, untie, or break that knot again,

Take me to you, imprison me, for I

Except you'enthrall me, never shall be free,

Nor ever chaste, except you ravish me.

GEORGE HERBERT (1593-1632)

John Donne dedicated his Holy Sonnets *to Herbert's mother, Lady Magdalen Herbert,*
an influential patron of the arts, and the young Herbert was friendly with both
Donne and Francis Bacon. At the age of seventeen he wrote to his mother from
Cambridge, announcing his intention of dedicating his poetry to God.
After a brief period as an MP during the 1620s, he returned to religious life and
devoted his few remaining years to it. When he contracted the illness which
killed him – tuberculosis – he sent his unpublished poems to his friend Nicholas Ferrar,
with the request that he publish the work if he thought that it might 'turn to the
advantage of any dejected soul'. Ferrar punctiliously carried out this last request and
most of Herbert's English poems appeared in a collection entitled The Temple *in 1633.*

DISCIPLINE

Throw away Thy rod,

Throw away Thy wrath

O my God,
Take the gentle path!

For my heart's desire
Unto Thine is bent:
I aspire
To a full consent.

Not a word or look
I affect to own,
But by book,
And Thy Book alone.

Though I fail, I weep;
Though I halt in pace,
Yet I creep
To the Throne of Grace.

Then let wrath remove;
Love will do the deed:
For with Love
Stony hearts will bleed.

Love is swift of foot;
Love's a man of war,
And can shoot,
And can hit from far.

Who can 'scape his bow?
That which wrought on Thee,

Brought Thee low,

Needs must work on me.

Throw away Thy rod;

Though man frailties hath,

Thou art God:

Throw away Thy wrath!

JOHN MILTON (1608-1674)

One of England's greatest poets, Milton seems to have led a blameless early career, committed to God and to poetry, written in Latin, Italian and English. He published his great elegy, Lycidas, *in 1936, but no further major works for twenty years. His fortunes took a more controversial turn with the outbreak of the Civil War, when he vociferously espoused the Cromwellian cause and wrote a number of pamphlets denouncing the power of the bishops. Over the next few years he also produced outspoken pamphlets on divorce, education and contemporary politics. After the Restoration of the monarchy in 1660, worn out by personal tragedy and the affliction of blindness, Milton retired from public life and devoted his time once again to poetry. In addition to* Lycidas, *the epics* Paradise Lost *and* Paradise Regained *and the tragedy* Samson Agonistes, *he penned a number of deeply moving shorter poems, notably the sonnet* On His Blindness.

ON HIS BLINDNESS

When I consider how my light is spent,

Ere half my days, in this dark world and wide,

And that one Talent which is death to hide,
Lodg'd with me useless, though my Soul more bent
To serve therewith my Maker, and present
My true account, least he returning chide,
Doth God exact day-labour, light deny'd,
I fondly ask; But patience to prevent
That murmur, soon replies, God doth not need
Either man's work or his own gifts, who best
Bear his milde yoak, they serve him best, his State
Is Kingly. Thousands at his bidding speed
And post o're Land and Ocean without rest:
They also serve who only stand and wait.

AT A SOLEMN MUSIC

Blest pair of Sirens, pledges of heaven's joy,
Sphere-born harmonious sisters, Voice and Verse,
Wed your divine sounds, and mixed power employ
Dead things with inbreathed sense able to pierce,
And to our high-raised phantasy present
That undisturbed song of pure consent,
Aye sung before the sapphire-coloured throne
To him that sits thereon,
With saintly shout and solemn jubilee,
Where the bright Seraphim in burning row
Their loud uplifted angel-trumpets blow,
And the Cherubic host in thousand quires
Touch their immortal harps of golden wires,
With those just spirits that wear victorious palms,

Hymns devout and holy psalms
Singing everlastingly;
That we on earth with undiscording voice
May rightly answer that melodious noise;
As once we did, till disproportioned sin
Jarred against Nature's chime, and with harsh din
Broke the fair music that all creatures made
To their great Lord, whose love their motion swayed
In perfect diapason, whilst they stood
In first obedience and their state of good.
O may we soon again renew that song,
And keep in tune with heaven, till God ere long
To his celestial consort us unite,
To live with him, and sing in endless morn of light.

HYMN TO LIGHT (from *Paradise Lost*)

Hail holy Light, offspring of Heav'n first-born,
Or of th'Eternal Coeternal beam
May I express thee unblam'd? since God is Light,
And never but in unapproached Light
Dwelt from Eternitie, dwelt then in thee,
Bright effluence of bright essence increate.
Or hear'st thou rather pure Ethereal stream,
Whose Fountain who shall tell? before the Sun,
Before the Heav'ns thou wert, and at the voice
Of God, as with a Mantle didst invest
The rising world of waters dark and deep,
Won from the void and formless infinite.

Thee I re-visit now with bolder wing,

Escap't the Stygian Pool, though long detained

In that obscure sojourn, while in my flight

Through utter and through middle darkness borne

With other notes than to th'Orphean Lyre

I sung of Chaos and Eternal Night.

ANNE BRADSTREET (1612-1672)

Considered 'the first American poet', Anne Bradstreet was born in England and
emigrated with her husband to the New World, where he became Governor of
Massachusetts. A devout Puritan, she wrote a large number of poems
concentrating more on the next world than on this.
Contemplations, *from which these extracts are taken,*
is probably her greatest work.

CONTEMPLATIONS (EXTRACTS)

II

I wist not what to wish, yet sure thought I,

If so much excellence abide below;

How excellent is he that dwells on high?

Whose power and beauty by his works we know,

Sure he is goodness, wisdom, glory, light,

That hath this under world so richly dight:

More Heaven than Earth was here no winter and no night.

XVIII

When I behold the heavens as in their prime,

And then the earth (though old) still clad in green,

The stones and trees, insensible of time,

Nor age nor wrinkle on their front are seen;

If winter come, and greenness then do fade,

A Spring returns, and they more youthful made;

But Man grows old, lies down, remains where once he's laid.

HENRY VAUGHAN (1621-1695)

Like John Donne, Vaughan produced satirical verses during the early part of his career,
before turning to religious poetry. It is thought that a combination of the Royalist defeat

in the Civil War and the premature death of his younger brother William may have led to the religious conversion that inspired this work.

PEACE

My soul, there is a country
Far beyond the stars,
Where stands a wingèd sentry
All skilful in the wars:

There, above noise and danger,
Sweet Peace sits crown'd with smiles,
And One born in a manger
Commands the beauteous files.

He is thy gracious Friend,
And – O my soul awake –
Did in pure love descend
To die here for thy sake.

If thou canst get but thither,
There grows the flower of Peace,
The Rose that cannot wither,
Thy fortress, and thy ease.

Leave then thy foolish ranges;
For none can thee secure
But One who never changes
Thy God, thy life, thy cure.

SPIRITUAL POETRY

THE NIGHT
(John 2. 3)

Through that pure Virgin-shrine,
That sacred veil drawn o'er thy glorious noon
That men might look and live as Glow-worms shine,
And face the Moon:
Wise Nicodemus saw such light
As made him know his God by night.

Were all my loud, evil days
Calm and unhaunted as is thy dark Tent,
Whose peace but by some Angel's wing or voice

Is seldom rent;

Then I in Heaven all the long year

Would keep, and never wander here.

But living where the Sun

Doth all things wake, and where all mix and tyre

Themselves and others, I consent and run

To ev'ry myre,

And by this world's ill-guiding light,

Err more than I can do by night.

There is in God (some say)

A deep, but dazzling darkness; as men here

Say it is late and dusky, because they

See not all clear;

O for that night! where I in him

Might live invisible and dim.

JOHN BUNYAN (1628-1688)

Religion was a controversial subject in England in the seventeenth century and Bunyan spent twelve years in prison for preaching without a licence. He was released in 1672, after the passing of the Declaration of Indulgence which allowed him to become a licensed preacher, but when this declaration was revoked the following year he again found himself behind bars. It was during this second period of imprisonment that he began his great work, The Pilgrim's Progress. *He is nowadays admired chiefly for his plain but beautiful prose style, but this poem remains a popular and rousing hymn.*

THE PILGRIM SONG

Who would true valour see
Let him come hither.
One here will constant be
Come wind, come weather.
There's no discouragement
Will make him once relent
His first avowed intent
To be a pilgrim.

Whoso beset him round
With dismal stories
Do but themselves confound:
His strength the more is.
No lion can him fright,
He'll with a giant fight,
But he will have a right
To be a pilgrim.

Hobgoblin nor foul fiend
Can daunt his spirit;
He knows he at the end
Shall life inherit.
Then fancies fly away,
He'll fear not what men say,
He'll labour night and day
To be a pilgrim.

SPIRITUAL POETRY

JOSEPH ADDISON (1672-1719)

Best remembered today as the co-founder of the Spectator *magazine and as a member
of a literary circle that included Jonathan Swift and Alexander Pope, Addison
was a distinguished classical scholar who, like many of his contemporaries, wrote a
number of his early works in Latin. His clear, approachable prose style, much admired by
Dr Johnson, enabled him to bring serious philosophical subjects to a wider audience and
is reflected in the straightforward language of this hymn.*

HYMN

The spacious firmament on high,
With all the blue ethereal sky,
And spangled heavens, a shining frame,
Their great Original proclaim.
Th'unwearied Sun from day to day
Does his Creator's power display;
And publishes to every land
The work of an Almighty hand.
Soon as the evening shades prevail.
The Moon takes up the wondrous tale;
And nightly to the listening Earth
Repeats the story of her birth:
Whilst all the stars that round her burn,
And all the planets in their turn,
Confirm the tidings as they roll,
And spread the truth from pole to pole.

What though in solemn silence all
Move round the dark terrestrial ball;

What though nor real voice nor sound
Amidst their radiant orbs be found
In Reason's ear they all rejoice,
And utter forth a glorious voice;
For ever singing as they shine,
'The Hand that made us is divine.'

ALEXANDER POPE (1688-1744)

Pope belongs to the Neo-Classical movement of poets who had rediscovered the virtues of the Greek and Latin writers and emulated their style. Much of his work was satirical, inspired by the Roman poet Horace, and he was not above including scandalous and recognisable verbal caricatures – a practice which lost him many friends in the course of his life. This poem finds him in an unusually reflective mood.

THE DYING CHRISTIAN TO HIS SOUL

Vital spark of heav'nly flame!
Quit, O quit this mortal frame:
Trembling, hoping, ling'ring, flying,
O the pain, the bliss of dying!
Cease, fond Nature, cease thy strife,
And let me languish into life.

Hark! they whisper; angels say,
Sister Spirit, come away!
What is this absorbs me quite?

Steals my senses, shuts my sight,
Drowns my spirits, draws my breath?
Tell me, my soul, can this be death?

The world recedes; it disappears!
Heav'n opens on my eyes! my ears
With sounds seraphic ring!
Lend, lend your wings! I mount! I fly!
Grave! where is thy victory?
O Death! where is thy sting?

CHARLES WESLEY (1707-1788)

Charles Wesley's elder brother John was the founder of the devout Christian group known as the Methodists. Charles followed his brother on some of his travels, notably to Moravia in eastern Europe, but although what they saw there had a profound influence on John's beliefs, Charles remained a member of the Church of England. He was probably England's most prolific composer of hymns, with several thousand to his credit.

MORNING HYMN

Christ, whose Glory fills the Skies,
Christ, the true, the only Light,
Sun of Righteousness, arise,
Triumph o'er the Shades of Night:
Day-spring from on High, be near:
Day-star, in my Heart appear.

Dark and Cheerless is the Morn
Unaccompanied by Thee,
Joyless is the Day's Return,
Till Thy Mercy's Beams I see;
Till they Inward Light impart,
Glad my Eyes, and warm my Heart.

Visit then this Soul of mine,
Pierce the Gloom of Sin and Grief,
Fill me, Radiancy Divine,
Scatter all my Unbelief,
More and more Thyself display
Shining to the Perfect Day.

ANNA LAETITIA BARBAULD (1743-1825)

Having published a successful collection of poems with her brother, John Aikin, Anna married a non-conformist minister and began moving in radical intellectual circles. She wrote various poems in support of their causes, as well as a great deal of popular work for children.

LIFE

Life! I know not what thou art,
But know that thou and I must part;
And when, or how, or where we met,
I own to me's a secret yet.

But this I know, when thou art fled,
Where'er they lay these limbs, this head,
No clod so valueless shall be
As all that then remains of me.

O whither, whither dost thou fly?
Where bend unseen thy trackless course?
And in this strange divorce,
Ah, tell where I must seek this compound I?
To the vast ocean of empyreal flame
From whence thy essence came
Dost thou thy flight pursue, when freed
From matter's base encumbering weed?
Or dost thou, hid from sight,
Wait, like some spell-bound knight,
Through blank oblivious years th'appointed hour
To break thy trance and reassume thy power?
Yet canst thou without thought or feeling be?
O say, what art thou, when no more thou'rt thee?

Life! we have been long together,
Through pleasant and through cloudy weather;
'Tis hard to part when friends are dear;
Perhaps 'twill cost a sigh, a tear;–
Then steal away, give little warning,
Choose thine own time;
Say not Good-night, but in some brighter clime
Bid me Good-morning!

SPIRITUAL POETRY

WILLIAM BLAKE (1757-1827)

Blake is one of the great mystical poets, seeing everything in nature as an embodiment of the divine. He rejected both the fashionable emphasis on materialism and the shackles of conventional Christianity in order to evolve a philosophy all his own. His poetry has moments of great lyricism and, in the eyes of many people, he will be for ever associated with the hymn Jerusalem, *but the poem reproduced below, is another perennial favourite.*

AUGURIES OF INNOCENCE (EXTRACT)

To see a World in a grain of sand,
And a Heaven in a wild flower,
Hold infinity in the palm of your hand,
And Eternity in an hour…
The bat that flits at close of eve
Has left the brain that won't believe.
The owl that calls upon the night
Speaks the unbeliever's fright…

Joy and woe are woven fine,
A clothing for the soul divine;
Under every grief and pine
Runs a joy with silken twine…

Every tear from every eye
Becomes a babe in Eternity…
The bleat, the bark, bellow and roar
Are waves that beat on Heaven's shore…
He who doubts from what he sees

Will ne'er believe, do what you please.
If the Sun and Moon should doubt,
They'd immediately go out…

God appears, and God is Light,
To those poor souls who dwell in Night;
But does a Human Form display
To those who dwell in realms of Day.

SAMUEL ROGERS (1763-1855)

A popular poet in his day, Rogers was particularly admired by Byron. His best known work, The Pleasures of Memory, *went through nineteen editions between 1792 and*

1816. In addition, he earned an excellent living as a banker and was sufficiently wealthy to be both an art collector and a generous patron of less successful poets.

A Wish

Mine be a cot beside the hill;
A bee-hive's hum shall soothe my ear;
A willowy brook, that turns a mill,
With many a fall shall linger near.

The swallow oft beneath my thatch
Shall twitter from her clay-built nest;
Oft shall the pilgrim lift the latch
And share my meal, a welcome guest.

Around my ivied porch shall spring
Each fragrant flower that drinks the dew;
And Lucy at her wheel shall sing
In russet gown and apron blue.

The village church among the trees,
Where first our marriage vows were given,
With merry peals shall swell the breeze
And point with taper spire to Heaven.

Samuel Taylor Coleridge (1772-1834)

With his friend William Wordsworth, Coleridge embodies the early part of the Romantic movement, whose mantle was later taken up by Byron, Keats and Shelley. An indefatigable traveller, he spent his most productive working periods in the Quantock Hills of Somerset and later in the Lake District, but also travelled extensively in Europe. His great works are The Rime of the Ancient Mariner *and* Kubla Khan, *the latter of which is said to have been inspired by an opium-induced dream. Coleridge was an emotionally unstable man who eventually quarrelled with many of his closest friends, but he produced arguably the finest poetry of his generation.*

THE PAINS OF SLEEP (EXTRACT)

Here on my bed my limbs I lay,
It hath not been my use to pray
With moving lips or bended knees;
But silently, by slow degrees,
My spirit I to Love compose,
In humble trust mine eye-lids close,
With reverential resignation,
No wish conceived, no thought exprest,
Only a sense of supplication;
A sense o'er all my soul imprest
That I am weak, yet not unblest,
Since in me, round me, every where
Eternal Strength and Wisdom are.

SELF-KNOWLEDGE

Know yourself – and is this the prime
And heaven-sprung adage of the olden time! –
Say, canst thou make thyself? – Learn first that trade; –

Haply thou mayst know what thyself had made,

What hast thou, Man, that thou dar'st call thine own? –

What is there in thee, Man, that canst be known? –

Dark fluxion, all unfixable by thought,

A phantom dim of past and future wrought,

Vain sister of the worm, – life, death, soul, clod –

Ignore thyself, and strive to know thy God.

JOHN KEATS (1795-1821)

One of the 'greats' of the second flowering of the Romantic period (see Coleridge, above) Keats died of tuberculosis at the age of 25, in the course of a visit to Italy. He had been ill for the last two years of his life and had written comparatively little during this period – his greatest period of creativity occurred when he was about twenty. No change of fashion in the last two centuries has diminished his reputation, and we are left to wonder what he might have achieved had he been allotted a longer lifespan.

WHEN I HAVE FEARS THAT I MAY CEASE TO BE

When I have fears that I may cease to be

Before my pen has glean'd my teeming brain,

Before high-piled books, in charact'ry,

Hold like rich garners the full-ripen'd grain;

When I behold, upon the night's starr'd face,

Huge cloudy symbols of a high romance,

And feel that I may never live to trace

Their shadows, with the magic hand of chance;

And when I feel, fair creature of an hour!
That I shall never look upon thee more,
Never have relish in the faery power
Of unreflecting love;– then on the shore
Of the wide world I stand alone, and think,
Till Love and Fame to nothingness do sink.

LAST SONNET

Bright Star, would I were steadfast as thou art –
Not in lone splendour hung aloft the night,
And watching, with eternal lids apart,
Like Nature's patient sleepless Eremite,
The moving waters at their priest-like task
Of pure ablution round earth's human shores,
Or gazing on the new soft-fallen mask
Of snow upon the mountains and the moors –
No – yet still steadfast, still unchangeable,
Pillow'd upon my fair love's ripening breast,
To feel for ever its soft fall and swell,
Awake for ever in a sweet unrest,
Still, still to hear her tender-taken breath,
And so live ever – or else swoon to death.

SPIRITUAL POETRY

FELICIA HEMANS (1793-1835)

The most popular female poet of her day, Felicia Hemans attracted the ardent attention of Shelley after her first volume of verse was published when she was fourteen. She won the Royal Society of Literature award in 1821 and, despite declining health, she continued to write, increasingly on religious subjects.

TO A FAMILY BIBLE

What household thoughts around thee, as their shrine,

Cling reverently? – of anxious looks beguiled,

My mother's eyes, upon thy page divine,

Each day were bent – her accents gravely mild,

Breathed out thy love: whilst I, a dreamy child,

Wandered on breeze-like fancies oft away,

To some lone tuft of gleaming spring-flowers wild,

Some fresh discover'd nook for woodland play,

Some secret nest: yet would the solemn Word

At times, with kindlings of young wonder heard,

Fall on my wakened spirit, there to be

A seed not lost; – for which, in darker years,

O Book of Heaven! I pour, with grateful tears,

Heart blessings on the holy dead and thee!

J. J. CALLANAN (1795-1829)

Despite the brevity of his life, the Irishman J. J. Callanan found time to study for the priesthood and then medicine, to become a soldier and, after selling out of the army, to

take up teaching. He collected and translated many early Irish legends and poems,
as well as writing his own verse, which won him two prizes from
Trinity College Dublin. He died of tuberculosis.

LINES TO THE BLESSED SACRAMENT

Thou dear and mystic semblance,
Before whose form I kneel,

I tremble as I think upon
The glory thou dost veil,
And ask myself can he who late
The ways of darkness trod,
Meet face to face, and heart to heart
His sin-avenging God?

My Judge and my Creator,
If I presume to stand
Amid thy pure and holy ones
It is at thy command,
To lay before thy mercy's seat
My sorrows and my fears,
To wail my life and kiss thy feet
In silence and in tears.

O God! that dreadful moment,
In sickness and in strife,
When death and hell seem'd watching
For the last weak pulse of life,
When on the waves of sin and pain
My drowning soul was toss'd,
Thy hand of mercy saved me then,
When hope itself was lost.

I hear thy voice, my Saviour,
It speaks within my breast,
'Oh, come to me, thou weary one,
I'll hush thy cares to rest;'

Then from the parch'd and burning waste
Of sin, where long I trod,
I come to thee, thou stream of life,
My Saviour and my God!

&⋅&

Throughout the eighteenth and nineteenth centuries, slaves on the plantations of the southern United States sought relief from unceasing toil and the uncertainty of their lives in deeply held religious beliefs which found expression in spontaneous singing. These songs formed a rich oral tradition and became known as 'negro spirituals'. The tunes of these compositions were born of the dual influence of Christian hymns and the rhythms brought over by the slaves from their native Africa. The forerunners of modern 'gospel' music, spirituals usually begin with a lead singer singing a line or short verse and the rest of the group joining in the chorus. Spirituals often speak of the singer's hope of salvation and happiness in the next world, contrasting it with the miseries of the present.

GIVE ME JESUS (*anon*)

Oh when I come to die
Oh when I come to die
Oh when I come to die
Give me Jesus
Give me Jesus
You may have the world
Give me Jesus

I heard my mother say
I heard my mother say

I heard my mother say

Give me Jesus

Give me Jesus

You may have the world

Give me Jesus

Dark midnight was my cry

Dark midnight was my cry

Dark midnight was my cry

Give me Jesus

Give me Jesus

You may have the world

Give me Jesus

In the morning when I rise

In the morning when I rise

In the morning when I rise

Give me Jesus

Give me Jesus

You may have the world

Give me Jesus

I heard the mourner say

I heard the mourner say

I heard the mourner say

Give me Jesus

Give me Jesus

You may have the world

Give me Jesus

SPIRITUAL POETRY

HARRIET MARTINEAU (1802-1876)

The daughter of an educated but impoverished family, Harriet Martineau began to write at an early age. By the time she was in her twenties she had converted to Unitarianism and was writing – and winning prizes for – essays on religious subjects. As her career progressed, she earned considerable sums of money and moved in literary circles, where she numbered the Wordsworths among her friends. But she continued to write on social issues and, after a visit to the United States, became an advocate for the abolition of slavery. Her few poems combine deep religious belief with the clear-sighted intelligence that characterises her other writing.

'ARISE, MY SOUL! AND URGE THY FLIGHT'

I

Arise, my soul! and urge thy flight,
And fix thy view on God alone,
As eagles spring to meet the light,
And gaze upon the radiant sun.

As planets on and onward roll,
As streams pour forth their swelling tide,
Press on thy steady course, my soul,
Nor pause, nor stop, nor turn aside.

Planets and suns shall dim their fire;
Earth, air and sea, shall melt away;
But though each star of heaven expire,
Thou may'st survive that awful day.

In life, in death, thy course hold on:

Though nature's self in ruins lie,

Pause not till heaven-gate be won;

Then rest; for there thou canst not die.

II

Beneath this starry arch

Nought resteth or is still;

But all things hold their march,

As if by one great will:

Moves one, move all;

Hark to the footfall!

On, on, for ever!

Yon sheaves were once but seed:

Will ripens into deed.

As cave-drops swell the streams,

Day-thoughts feed nightly dreams;

And sorrow tracketh wrong,

As echo follows song.

On, on, for ever!

By night, like stars on high,

The hours reveal their train;

They whisper, and go by;

I never watch in vain:

Moves one, move all:

Hark to the footfall!

On, on, for ever!

They pass the cradle-head,
And there a promise shed;
They pass the moist new grave,
And bid rank verdure wave;
They bear through every clime
The harvests of all time,
On, on, for ever!

III

All men are equal in their birth,
Heirs of the earth and skies;
All men are equal when that earth
Fades from their dying eyes.

All wait alike on Him whose power
Upholds the life He gave;
The sage within his star-lit tower,
The savage in his cave.

God meets the throngs that pay their vows
In courts their hands have made;
And hears the worshipper who bows
Beneath the plantain shade.

'Tis man alone who difference sees,
And speaks of high and low,
And worships those and tramples these,
While the same path they go.

Oh, let man hasten to restore

To all their rights of love;

In power and wealth exult no more;

In wisdom lowly move.

Ye great! renounce your earth-born pride;

Ye low, your shame and fear:

Live as ye worship side by side;

Your brotherhood revere.

VICTOR HUGO (1802-1885)

Although Hugo is best known in the English-speaking world for his novels Les
Misérables *and* The Hunchback of Notre-Dame, *he is regarded by many as the finest
poet France has produced. In addition to writing, he had an active political career.
Objecting to the* coup d'etat *of 1851 which formed the Second Empire under Napoleon
III, he went into exile in the Channel Islands, returning only after the republic was
restored. He had by this time established such a reputation that he found himself a
national figure, was elected a senator and, after his death, awarded a state funeral.*

THE POET'S SIMPLE FAITH

You say, 'Where goest thou?' I cannot tell,

And still go on. If but the way be straight,

It cannot go amiss! before me lies

Dawn and the Day; the Night behind me; that

Suffices me; I break the bounds; I *see*,

And nothing more; *believe*, and nothing less.

My future is not one of my concerns.

GERALD GRIFFIN (1803-1840)

Born and raised in Limerick, Griffin moved to London when the failure of their brewing business caused the rest of his family to emigrate to America. He scraped a living as a journalist before finding recognition through his stories and poems, which were much admired by Tennyson. Unimpressed by success, he returned to Ireland, joined the Society of the Christian Brothers and spent the last two years of his life teaching in their service.

TO THE BLESSED VIRGIN MARY

As the mute nightingale in closest groves

Lies hid at noon, but when day's piercing eye

Is locked in night, with full heart beating high,

Poureth her plain song o'er the light she loves,

So, Virgin, ever pure and ever blest,

Moon of religion, from whose radiant face,

Reflected, streams the light of heavenly grace

On broken hearts, by contrite thoughts oppressed –

So, Mary, they who justly feel the weight

Of Heaven's offended majesty, implore

Thy reconciling aid, with suppliant knee.

Of sinful man, O sinless Advocate!

To thee they turn, nor him the less adore;

'Tis still his light they love, less dreadful seen in thee.

SPIRITUAL POETRY

ELIZABETH BARRETT BROWNING (1806-1861)

The love affair between Elizabeth Barrett and Robert Browning was a scandal in its day and remains fixed in the public imagination as one of history's great romances. Defying her overbearing father, the couple eloped to Italy and spent the rest of her life there, entertaining literary friends and becoming involved in the campaign for the unification of Italy. During her lifetime, Elizabeth was regarded as a greater poet than her husband and was even considered for the position of Poet Laureate (a post which has to this day never been held by a woman).

CONSOLATION

All are not taken; there are left behind
Living Beloveds, tender looks to bring
And make the daylight still a happy thing,
And tender voices, to make soft the wind:
But if it were not so – if I could find
No love in all the world for comforting,
Nor any path but hollowly did ring
Where 'dust to dust' the love from life disjoined,
And if, before those sepulchres unmoving
I stood alone (as some forsaken lamb
Goes bleating up the moors in weary dearth),
Crying, 'Where are ye, O my loved and loving?' –
I know a Voice would sound, 'Daughter, I AM.
Can I suffice for HEAVEN and not for earth?'

LIFE

Each creature holds an insular point in space;

Yet what man stirs a finger, breathes a sound,

But all the multitudinous beings round

In all the countless worlds with time and place

For their conditions, down to the central base,

Thrill, haply, in vibration and rebound,

Life answering life across the vast profound,

In full antiphony, by a common grace?

I think this sudden joyaunce which illumes

A child's mouth sleeping, unaware may run

From some soul newly loosened from earth's tombs:

I think this passionate sigh, which half-begun

I stifle back, may reach and stir the plumes

Of God's calm angel standing in the sun.

RICHARD MONCKTON MILNES, BARON HOUGHTON (1809-1885)

Richard Milnes was a career politician who was also a great patron of the arts.
He befriended Tennyson, Hallam and Thackeray at Cambridge; he later
became a champion of Blake and of Keats, whose Life *and* Letters *he published.*
In 1850, on the death of Wordsworth, he was instrumental in having Tennyson
appointed Poet Laureate. As for his own writing, in addition to verse, he produced works
of biography, history and sociology. Politically, one of his great achievements
concerned the first Copyright Act.

SPIRITUAL POETRY

THE MEN OF OLD

I know not that the men of old
Were better than men now,
Of heart more kind, of hand more bold,
Of more ingenuous brow:
I heed not those who pine for force
A ghost of Time to raise,
As if they thus could check the course
Of these appointed days.

Still it is true, and over true,
That I delight to close
This book of life self-wise and new,
And let my thoughts repose

On all that humble happiness
The world has since forgone,
The daylight of contentedness
That on those faces shone.

With rights, tho' not too closely scanned
Enjoy'd as far as known;
With will by no reverse unmann'd,
With pulse of even tone,
They from to-day and from to-night
Expected nothing more
Than yesterday and yesternight
Had proffer'd them before.

To them was Life a simple art
Of duties to be done,
A game where each man took his part
A race where all must run;
A battle whose great scheme and scope
They little cared to know,
Content as men-at-arms to cope
Each with his fronting foe.

Man now his Virtue's diadem
Puts on and proudly wears:
Great thoughts, great feelings came to them
Like instincts, unawares.
Blending their souls' sublimest needs
With tasks of every day,
They went about their gravest deeds
As noble boys at play.

SPIRITUAL POETRY

Alfred, Lord Tennyson (1809-1892)

*The great poetic figure of the nineteenth century, Tennyson was Poet Laureate for over
forty years and influenced every versifier of the next generation. In the 1850s he moved
to Farringford on the Isle of Wight, where he spent most of the rest of his life
and held court for visiting writers such as William Allingham, Edward Lear and
Coventry Patmore. He was immensely prolific and wrote on a wide
variety of themes, historical, spiritual and personal.*

The Higher Pantheism

The sun, the moon, the stars, the seas, the hills and the plains –
Are not these, O Soul, the Vision of Him who reigns?

Is not the Vision He? tho' He be not that which He seems?
Dreams are true while they last, and do we not live in dreams?

Earth, these solid stars, this weight of body and limb,
Are they not sign and symbol of thy division from Him?

Dark is the world to thee: thyself art the reason why;
For is He not all but that which has power to feel 'I am I'?

Glory about thee, without thee; and thou fulfillest thy doom
Making Him broken gleams, and a stifled splendour and gloom.

Speak to Him thou for He hears, and Spirit with Spirit can meet –
Closer is He than breathing, and nearer than hands and feet.

God is law, say the wise; O Soul, and let us rejoice,
For if He thunder by law the thunder is yet His voice.

Law is God, say some: no God at all, says the fool;
For all we have power to see is a straight staff bent in a pool;

And the ear of man cannot hear, and the eye of man cannot see;
But if we could see and hear, this Vision – were it not He?

HENRY DAVID THOREAU (1817-1862)

Thoreau was one of the most influential figures in American literature in the mid-nineteenth century, largely due to his experiment in self-sufficiency at Walden, near his birthplace, Concord, Massachusetts. Thoreau lived at Walden for only two years before being drawn back to the materialistic world he claimed to despise, but his account of his experiences is a masterpiece of political and philosophical thought and of naturalistic prose. The inextricable relationship between nature and spirituality can also be seen in this poem.

THE MOON NOW RISES

The moon now rises to her absolute rule,
And the husbandman and hunter
Acknowledge her for their mistress.
Asters and golden reign in the fields
And the life everlasting withers not.
The fields are reaped and shorn of their pride

But an inward verdure still crowns them
The thistle scatters its down on the pool
And yellow leaves clothe the river –
And nought disturbs the serious life of men.
But behind the sheaves and under the sod
There lurks a ripe fruit which the reapers have not gathered
The true harvest of the year – the boreal fruit
Which it bears forever.
With fondness annually watering and maturing it.
But man never severs the stalk
Which bears this palatable fruit.

EMILY BRONTË (1818-1848)

*The greatest poet of her talented family, Emily Brontë was preoccupied with death from
an early age – hardly surprisingly, given that her two eldest sisters and her mother had
died by the time Emily was seven. With her sister Charlotte she went to Brussels
to study in 1842, but did not enjoy being away from the Yorkshire moors and returned
home ahead of the appointed time. She remained there for the rest of her life,
living in seclusion, apparently with few friends, but writing her best poetry.
The wild and violent landscape of her home inspired her as much
as did her fervent imagination.*

DEATH

Death! that struck when I was most confiding
In my certain faith of joy to be

Strike again, Time's withered branch dividing
From the fresh root of Eternity!

Leaves, upon Time's branch, were growing brightly,
Full of sap, and full of silver-dew;
Birds beneath its shelter gathered nightly;
Daily round its flowers the wild bees flew.

Sorrow passed, and plucked the golden blossom;
Guilt stripped off the foliage in its pride;
But, within its parent's kindly bosom,
Flowed for ever Life's restoring tide.

Little mourned I for the parted gladness,
For the vacant nest and silent song
Hope was there, and laughed me out of sadness,
Whispering, 'Winter will not linger long!'

And, behold! with tenfold increase blessing,
Spring adorned the beauty-burdened spray;
Wind and rain and fervent heat, caressing,
Lavished glory on that second May!

High it rose – no wingèd grief could sweep it;
Sin was scared to distance with its shine;
Love, and its own life, had power to keep it
From all wrong – from every blight but thine!

Cruel Death! The young leaves droop and languish;
Evening's gentle air may still restore.

No! the morning sunshine mocks my anguish
Time, for me, must never blossom more!

Strike it down, that other boughs may flourish
Where that perished sapling used to be;
Thus, at least, its mouldering corpse will nourish
That from which it sprung – Eternity.

'HOW BEAUTIFUL THE EARTH IS STILL'

How beautiful the Earth is still
To thee – how full of Happiness;
How little fraught with real ill
Or shadowy phantoms of distress;

How Spring can bring thee glory yet
And Summer win thee to forget
December's sullen time!
Why dost thou hold the treasure fast
Of youth's delight, when youth is past
And thou art near thy prime?

When those who were thy own compeers,
Equal in fortunes and in years,
Have seen their morning melt in tears,
To dull unlovely day;

Blest, had they died unproved and young
Before their hearts were wildly wrung,

Poor slaves, subdued by passions strong,
A weak and helpless prey!

'Because, I hoped while they enjoyed,
And by fulfilment, hope destroyed –
As children hope, with trustful breast,
I waited Bliss and cherished Rest.

'A thoughtful Spirit taught me soon
That we must long till life be done;
That every phase of earthly joy
Will always fade and always cloy –

'This I foresaw, and would not chase
The fleeting treacheries,
But with firm foot and tranquil face
Held backward from the tempting race,
Gazed o'er the sands the waves efface
To the enduring seas –

'There cast my anchor of Desire
Deep in unknown Eternity;
Nor ever let my Spirit tire
With looking for what is to be.

'It is Hope's spell that glorifies
Like youth to my maturer eyes
All Nature's million mysteries –
The fearful and the fair –

'Hope soothes me in the griefs I know,
She lulls my pain for others' woe
And makes me strong to undergo
What I am born to bear.

'Glad comforter, will I not brave
Unawed the darkness of the grave?
Nay, smile to hear Death's billows rave,
My Guide, sustained by thee?

'The more unjust seems present fate
The more my Spirit springs elate
Strong in thy strength, to anticipate
Rewarding Destiny!'

'FAIR SINKS THE SUMMER EVENING NOW'

Fair sinks the summer evening now
In softened glory round my home;
The sky upon its holy brow
Wears not a cloud that speaks of gloom.

The old tower, shrined in golden light,
Looks down on the descending sun;
So gently evening blends with night,
You scarce can say that day is done.

And this is just the joyous hour
When we were wont to burst away,

To 'scape from labour's tyrant power
And cheerfully go out to play.

Then why is all so sad and lone?
No merry foot-step on the stair;
No laugh – no heart-awaking tone,
But voiceless silence everywhere?

I've wandered round our garden-ground,
And still it seemed at every turn
That I should greet approaching feet,
And words upon the breezes borne.

In vain – they will not come to-day;
And morning's beam will rise as drear:
Then tell me – are they gone for aye?
Our sun blinks through the mists of care.

'Ah no,' reproving hope doth say,
'Departed joys 'tis fond to mourn
When every storm that rides this way
Prepares a more divine return.'

ARTHUR HUGH CLOUGH (1819-1861)

Arthur Clough was born in Liverpool but went to America as a small child with his merchant father. Sent back to England to school and to Oxford University, he found himself in conflict with the Thirty-Nine Articles which are the basic tenets of the Anglican clergy. He became generally anti-establishment in his views, describing himself as a republican and deploring the class system and capitalism.

There Is No God

'There is no God,' the wicked saith,
'And truly it's a blessing,
For what he might have done with us
It's better only guessing.'

'There is no God,' a youngster thinks,
'Or really, if there may be,
He surely didn't mean a man
Always to be a baby.'

'There is no God, or if there is,'
The tradesman thinks, ''twere funny
If he should take it ill in me
To make a little money.'

'Whether there be,' the rich man says,
'It matters very little,
For I and mine, thank somebody,
Are not in want of victual.'

Some others, also, to themselves
Who scarce so much as doubt it,
Think there is none, when they are well,
And do not think about it.

But country folks who live beneath
The shadow of the steeple;

SPIRITUAL POETRY

The parson and the parson's wife,
And mostly married people;

Youths green and happy in first love,
So thankful for illusion;
And men caught out in what the world
Calls guilt, in first confusion;

And almost everyone when age,
Disease, or sorrows strike him,
Inclines to think there is a God,
Or something very like him.

❧❧❧

SPIRITUAL POETRY

WALT WHITMAN (1819-1892)

The literary colossus of nineteenth-century America, Whitman aimed to include in his work 'the whole sphere of modern man'. This ambition led him to introduce a number of 'taboo' subjects, which sometimes lost him friends or jobs. His great work is
The Leaves of Grass, *which Ralph Waldo Emerson hailed as 'the most extraordinary piece of wit and wisdom that America has yet contributed'.*
Like Emerson and Thoreau, Whitman was eager to establish a voice for American poetry, unfettered by European influence. The long, irregular lines of this poem are characteristic of his style.

GRAND IS THE SEEN

Grand is the seen, the light, to me – grand are the sky and stars,
Grand is the earth, and grand are lasting time and space,
And grand their laws, so multiform, puzzling, evolutionary;
But grander far the unseen soul of me, comprehending, endowing all those,
Lighting the light, the sky and stars, delving the earth, sailing the sea,
(What were all those, indeed, without thee, unseen soul? of what amount
without thee?)
More evolutionary, vast, puzzling, O my soul!
More multiform far – more lasting thou than they.

ANNE BRONTË (1820-1849)

The youngest of the Brontë sisters, Anne was beset by doubts as to whether she was one of God's chosen, yet found it hard to believe that God could be so cruel as to reject

SPIRITUAL POETRY

creatures He Himself had created. These doubts and the bitterness and sorrow they engendered feature largely in her poetry.

A PRAYER

My God (oh, let me call Thee mine,
Weak, wretched sinner though I be),
My trembling soul would fain be Thine;
My feeble faith still clings to Thee.

Not only for the past I grieve,
The future fills me with dismay;
Unless Thou hasten to relieve,
Thy suppliant is a castaway.

I cannot say my faith is strong,
I dare not hope my love is great;

But strength and love to Thee belong:
Oh, do not leave me desolate!

I know I owe my all to Thee;
Oh, take the heart I cannot give;
Do Thou my Strength, my Saviour be,
And make me to Thy glory live!

THE DOUBTER'S PRAYER

Eternal Power, of earth and air!
Unseen, yet seen in all around,
Remote, but dwelling everywhere,
Though silent, heard in every sound.

If e'er Thine ear in mercy bent,
When wretched mortals cried to Thee,
And if, indeed, Thy Son was sent,
To save lost sinners such as me:

Then hear me now, while, kneeling here,
I lift to Thee my heart and eye,
And all my soul ascends in prayer,
Oh, give me – give me Faith! I cry.

Without some glimmering in my heart,
I could not raise this fervent prayer;
But, oh! a stronger light impart,
And in Thy mercy fix it there.

While Faith is with me, I am blest;
It turns my darkest night to day;
But while I clasp it to my breast,
I often feel it slide away.

Then, cold and dark, my spirit sinks,
To see my light of life depart;
And every fiend of Hell, methinks,
Enjoys the anguish of my heart.

What shall I do, if all my love,
My hopes, my toil, are cast away,
And if there be no God above,
To hear and bless me when I pray?

If this be vain delusion all,
If death be an eternal sleep,
And none can hear my secret call,
Or see the silent tears I weep!

Oh, help me, God! For Thou alone
Canst my distracted soul relieve;
Forsake it not: it is Thine own,
Though weak, yet longing to believe.

Oh, drive these cruel doubts away;
And make me know that Thou art God!
A faith, that shines by night and day,
Will lighten every earthly load.

If I believe that Jesus died,
And, waking, rose to reign above;
Then surely Sorrow, Sin, and Pride,
Must yield to Peace, and Hope, and Love.

And all the blessed words He said
Will strength and holy joy impart:
A shield of safety o'er my head,
A spring of comfort in my heart.

CHARLES BAUDELAIRE

Charles Baudelaire came from an affluent background but squandered his inheritance in extravagant living and ended his life in poverty and squalor. His great work, Les Fleurs du Mal, *far from restoring his fortunes, forced him into the law courts, where he was fined for offences to public morals and suffered the indignity of having six of the poems banned. His genius was recognised only posthumously. Baudelaire is now regarded as one of the great French writers and an important influence on the generations of poets who have followed him.*

THE SPIRITUAL DAWN (from *Les Fleurs du Mal*)

When upon revellers the stained dawn breaks
The fierce ideal comes with it; at that hour,
Stirred by some terrible avenging power,
An angel in the sated brute awakes.
Above the stricken, suffering man there glow

Far azure plains of unimagined bliss
Which draw his dreaming spirit like the abyss.
O pure, beloved Goddess, even so
Over smoked wrecks of stupid scenes of shame
Brighter and rosier thy sweet memory
Hovers before my wide eyes hauntingly.
The sun has dimmed and charred the candles' flame,
And thus, my glorious all-conquering one,
Thy shade is peer to the immortal Sun.

EMILY PFEIFFER (1827-1890)

Emily Pfeiffer produced her first volume of poems and stories when she was sixteen and continued to publish regularly throughout her life. Her early work is devotedly largely to the education of women and other issues related to women's rights. But there is always a strong undercurrent of Christianity, which becomes more prominent in her later verses.

THE 'STING OF DEATH'

O thou whom men affirm we cannot know,
It may be we may never see Thee nearer
Than 'in the clouds', nor ever trace Thee clearer
Than in that garment which, howe'er aglow
With love divine, is still a changing show,
A little shadowing forth, and more concealing,
A glory which, in uttermost revealing,
Might strike us dead with one supreme life-blow.

We may not reach Thee through the void immense

Measured by suns, or prove Thee anywhere,

But hungry eyes that hunt the wilds above

For one lost face, still drop despairing thence

To find Thee in the heart – life's ravished lair –

Else were the 'sting of death' not sin, but love!

CHRISTINA ROSSETTI (1830-1894)

The sister of the artist and poet Dante Gabriel Rossetti was closely allied to the Pre-Raphaelites and was engaged to the painter James Collinson. The engagement was broken off when he became a Catholic, as Christina was a staunch Anglican. She never married and much of her poetry is concerned with unrequited or frustrated love. Like Teresa of Avila (see page 43), Emily Dickinson (see page 119) and other female 'mystical' poets, she often uses the language of earthly love to convey spiritual passion.

MONNA INNOMINATA: A SONNET OF SONNETS (EXTRACT)

If I could trust mine own self with your fate,

Shall I not rather trust it in God's hand?

Without Whose Will one lily doth not stand,

Nor sparrow fall at his appointed date;

Who numbereth the innumerable sand,

Who weighs the wind and water with a weight,

To Whom the world is neither small nor great,

Whose knowledge foreknew every plan we planned.

Searching my heart for all that touches you,
I find there only love and love's goodwill
Helpless to help and impotent to do,
Of understanding dull, of sight most dim;

And therefore I commend you back to Him
Whose love your love's capacity can fill.

To What Purpose Is this Waste? (EXTRACT)

A windy shell singing upon the shore:
A lily budding in a desert place;
Blooming alone
With no companion
To praise its perfect perfume and its grace:
A rose crimson and blushing at the core,
Hedged in with thorns behind it and before.
A fountain in the grass,
Whose shadowy waters pass
Only to nourish birds and furnish food
For squirrels of the wood:
An oak deep in the forest's heart, the house
Of black-eyed tiny mouse
Its strong roots fit for fuel roofing in
The hoarded nuts, acorns and grains of wheat;
Shutting them from the wind and scorching heat,
And sheltering them when the rains begin:
A precious pearl deep buried in sea
Where none save fishes be:
The fullest merriest note
For which the skylark strains his silver throat,
Heard only in the sky
By other birds that fitfully
Chase one another as they fly:

The ripest plum down tumbled to the ground
By southern winds most musical of sound.
But by no thirsty traveller found:
Honey of wild bees in their ordered cells
Stored, not for human mouths to taste: –
I said, smiling superior down: What waste
Of good, where no man dwells.

This I said on a pleasant day in June
Before the sun had set, tho' a white moon

Already flaked the quiet blue
Which not a star looked thro'.
But still the air was warm, and drowsily
It blew into my face:
So since that same day I had wandered deep
Into the country, I sought out a place
For rest beneath a tree,
And very soon forgot myself in sleep:
Not so mine own words had forgotten me.
Mine eyes were opened to behold
All hidden things,
And mine ears heard all secret whisperings:
So my proud tongue that had been bold
To carp and to reprove,
Was silenced by the force of utter Love…

Why should we grudge a hidden water stream
To birds and squirrels while we have enough?
As if a nightingale should cease to sing
Lest we should hear, or finch leafed out of sight
Warbling its fill in summer light;
As if sweet violets in the spring
Should cease to blow, for fear our path should seem
Less weary or less rough.
So every oak that stands a house
For skilful mouse,
And year by year renews its strength
Shakes acorns from a hundred boughs
Which shall be oaks at length.

Who hath weighed the waters and shall say
What is hidden in the depths from day?
Pearls and precious stones and golden sands,
Wondrous weeds and blossoms rare,
Kept back from human hands,
But good and fair,
A silent praise as pain is silent prayer.
A hymn, an incense rising toward the skies,
As our whole life should rise;
An offering without stint from earth below,
Which Love accepteth so.

Thus is it with a warbling bird,
With fruit bloom-ripe and full of seed,
With honey which the wild bees draw
From flowers, and store for future need
By a perpetual law.
We want the faith that hath not seen
Indeed, but hath believed His truth
Who witnessed that His work was good:
So we pass cold to age from youth.
Alas for us: for we have heard
And known, but have not understood.

IF ONLY

If only I might love my God and die! –
But now He bids me love Him and live on,
Now when the bloom of all my life is gone,

The pleasant half of life has quite gone by.

My tree of hope is lopt that spread so high;

And I forget how summer glowed and shone,

While autumn grips me with its fingers wan,

And frets me with its fitful windy sigh.

When autumn passes then must winter numb,

And winter may not pass a weary while.

But when it passes spring shall flower again:

And in that spring who weepeth now shall smile –

Yea, they shall wax who now are on the wane,

Yea, they shall sing for love when Christ shall come.

T. E. BROWN (1830-1897)

Born on the Isle of Man, Thomas Edward Brown wrote largely in the Manx dialect.
This is his only well-known English poem.

MY GARDEN

A garden is a lovesome thing, God wot!

Rose plot,

Fringed pool,

Fern'd grot –

The veriest school

Of peace; and yet the fool

Contends that God is not –

Not God! in gardens! when the eve is cool?

SPIRITUAL POETRY

Nay, but I have a sign;
'Tis very sure God walks in mine.

EMILY DICKINSON (1830-1894)

*Much of Emily Dickinson's poetry was published posthumously, as the reclusive author
had not wished it to appear during her lifetime. Her work suggests that she was
disappointed with this world, more concerned with her love of God and
intrigued by the prospect of death.*

'I Took One Draught of Life'

I took one Draught of Life –
I'll tell you what I paid –
Precisely an existence –
The market price, they said.

They weighed me, Dust by Dust –
They balanced Film with Film,
Then handed me my Being's worth –
A single Dram of Heaven!

'It's Easy to Invent a Life'

It's easy to invent a Life –
God does it – every Day –
Creation – but the Gambol
Of His Authority –

It's easy to efface it –
The thrifty Deity
Could scarce afford Eternity
To Spontaneity –

The Perished Patterns murmur –
But His Perturbless Plan
Proceed – inserting Here – a Sun –
There – leaving out a Man.

APPARENTLY WITH NO SURPRISE'

Apparently with no surprise
To any happy Flower
The Frost beheads it at its play
In accidental power
The blonde Assassin passes on –
The Sun proceeds unmoved
To measure off another Day
For an Approving God.

STOPFORD A. BROOKE (1832-1916)

*The Irish-born Brooke was educated at Trinity College Dublin, was ordained as
a minister and became Chaplain in Ordinary to Queen Victoria in 1872. In 1880
he left the Anglican church to become a Unitarian. In addition to works of theology
he published a number of volumes of poetry and became President of the
Irish Literary Society of London in 1899.*

THE EARTH AND MAN

A little sun, a little rain,
A soft wind blowing from the west,
And woods and fields are sweet again,
And warmth within the mountain's breast.

So simple is the earth we tread,
So quick with love and life her frame,
Ten thousand years have dawned and fled,
And still her magic is the same.

A little love, a little trust,
A soft impulse, a sudden dream,
And life as dry as desert dust
Is fresher than a mountain stream.

So simple is the heart of man,
So ready for new hope and joy;
Ten thousand years since it began
Have left it younger than a boy.

GERARD MANLEY HOPKINS (1844-1889)

One critic has suggested that Hopkins' nature poems 'might not too rashly be interpreted as a deliberate campaign to Christianise the Romantic cult of nature'. Certainly Hopkins, who was a devout Jesuit, frequently uses nature as a way of praising God.

HEAVEN-HAVEN
(A nun takes the veil)

I have desired to go
Where springs not fail,
To fields where flies no sharp and sided hail

And a few lilies blow.
And I have asked to be
Where no storms come,
Where the green swell is in the havens dumb,
And out of the swing of the sea.

As Kingfishers Catch Fire

As kingfishers catch fire, dragonflies draw flame;
As tumbled over rim in roundy wells
Stones ring; like each tucked string tells, each hung bell's
Bow swung finds tongue to fling out broad its name;

Each mortal thing does one thing and the same;
Deals out that being indoors each one dwells;
Selves – goes its self: *myself* it speaks and spells,
Crying *What I do is me*; for that I came.

I say more: the just man justices;
Keeps grace; that keeps all his goings graces;
Acts in God's eye what in God's eye he is –
Christ. For Christ plays in ten thousand places,
Lovely in limbs, and lovely in eyes not his
To the Father through the features of men's faces.

ROBERT BRIDGES (1844-1930)

Bridges was deeply concerned with religious matters and this is reflected in his poetry, although not all of it is devotional. He became Poet Laureate in 1913 and what is arguably his best work – The Testament of Beauty *– was published in 1929 when he was already eighty-five years old. A life-long friend of Gerard Manley Hopkins, Bridges spent much of his later years editing and promoting Hopkins' poetry; he was instrumental in the publication of the latter's complete works in 1918.*

THE GROWTH OF LOVE (EXTRACTS)

VIII

For beauty being the best of all we know
Sums up the unsearchable and secret aims
Of nature, and on joys whose earthly names
Were never told can form and sense bestow:

And man hath sped his instinct to outgo
The step of science; and against her shames
Imagination stakes out heavenly claims,
Building a tower above the head of woe.

Nor is there fairer work for beauty found
Than that she win in nature her release
From all the woes that in the world abound:
Nay, with his sorrow may his love increase,
If from man's greater need beauty redound,
And claim his tears for homage of his peace.

XXXV

All earthly beauty hath one cause and proof,
To lead the pilgrim soul to beauty above:
Yet lieth the greater bliss so far aloof,
That few there be are wean'd from earthly love.
Joy's ladder it is, reaching from home to home,
The best of all the work that all was good;
Whereof 'twas writ the angels aye upclomb,
Down sped, and at the top the Lord God stood.

But I my time abuse, my eyes by day
Center'd on thee, by night my heart on fire –
Letting my number'd moments run away –
Nor e'en 'twixt night and day to heaven aspire:
So true it is that what the eye seeth not
But slow is loved, and loved is soon forgot.

SPIRITUAL POETRY

VIVEKANANDA (1862-1902)

The great Hindu philosopher of his generation, Vivekananda became a celebrity in America after attending the Parliament of Religions in Chicago in 1893, where he represented Hinduism and fired the public imagination with his eloquence, deep spiritual insight and colourful personality. He was an ardent advocate of a greater understanding between East and West. In India he is regarded as the inspiration behind modern nationalist feeling.

THE LIVING GOD

He who is in you and outside you,
Who works through all hands,
Who walks on all feet,
Whose body are all ye,
Him worship, and break all other idols!

He who is at once the high and low,
The sinner and the saint,
Both God and worm,
Him worship – visible, knowable, real, omnipresent.
Break all other idols!

In whom is neither past life
Nor future birth nor death,
In whom we always have been
And always shall be one,
Him worship. Break all other idols!

Ye fools! who neglect the living God,
And His infinite reflections with which the world is full,
While ye run after imaginary shadows,
That lead alone to fights and quarrels,
Him worship, the only visible!
Break all other idols!

REQUIESCAT IN PACE

Speed forth, O Soul! upon thy star-strewn path;
Speed, blissful one! where thought is ever free,
Where time and space no longer mist the view,
Eternal peace and blessings be with thee!

Thy service true complete thy sacrifice,
Thy home the heart of love transcendent find;
Remembrance sweet, that kills all space and time.
Like altar roses fill thy place behind!

Thy bonds are broke, thy quest in bliss is found,
And one with That which comes as Death and Life;
Thou helpful one! unselfish e'er on earth,
Ahead! still help with love this world of strife!

SPIRITUAL POETRY

ALICE MEYNELL (1847-1922)

Alice Meynell converted to Catholicism while in her teens and its teachings were a great influence on her life and work, which was initially modelled on the poems of Elizabeth Barrett Browning and Christina Rossetti. Like Elizabeth Barrett, she met her future husband, the author and editor Wilfrid Meynell, because he read and admired her poetry.

CHRIST IN THE UNIVERSE

With this ambiguous earth
His dealings have been told us. These abide:
The signal to a maid, the human birth,
The lesson, and the young Man crucified.

But not a star of all
The innumerable host of stars has heard
How He administered this terrestrial ball.
Our race have kept their Lord's entrusted Word.

Of His earth-visiting feet
None knows the secret, cherished, perilous,
The terrible, shamefast, frightened, whispered, sweet,
Heart-shattering secret of His way with us.

No planet knows that this
Our wayside planet, carrying land and wave,
Love and life multiplied, and pain and bliss,
Bears, as chief treasure, one forsaken grave.

Nor, in our little day,
May His devices with the heavens be guessed,
His pilgrimage to thread the Milky Way,
Or His bestowals there be manifest.

But, in the eternities,
Doubtless we shall compare together, hear
A million alien Gospels, in what guise
He trod the Pleiades, the Lyre, the Bear.

O be prepared, my soul!
To read the inconceivable, to scan
The million forms of God those stars unroll
When, in our turn, we show to them a Man:

VENI CREATOR

So humble things Thou hast borne for us, O God,
Left'st Thou a path of lowliness untrod?
Yes, one, till now; another Olive-Garden.
For we endure the tender pain of pardon –
One with another we forbear. Give heed,
Look at the mournful world Thou hast decreed.
The time has come. At last we hapless men
Know all our haplessness all through. Come, then,
Endure undreamed humility: Lord of Heaven,
Come to our ignorant hearts and be forgiven.

SPIRITUAL POETRY

ELLA WHEELER WILCOX (1850-1919)

Ella Wheeler Wilcox is remembered almost entirely for the first two lines of this poem, but in her day she was one of the most popular poets in America, having produced volumes of optimistic religious verse which touched the hearts of millions of people. One critic, remarking that her poetry is not really very good, says that she was 'no minor poet. Instead, she was a poor quality poet of major significance...who hit a public nerve better poets failed to touch at all.'

LAUGH, AND THE WORLD LAUGHS WITH YOU

Laugh, and the world laughs with you;
Weep, and you weep alone;
For this brave old earth must borrow its mirth,
It has trouble enough of its own.
Sing, and the hills will answer;
Sigh! it is lost on the air;
The echoes bound to a joyful sound,
But shrink from voicing care.

Rejoice, and men will seek you;
Grieve, and they turn and go;
They want full measure of all your pleasure,
But they do not want your woe.
Be glad, and your friends are many;
Be sad, and you lose them all
There are none to decline your nectared wine,
But alone you must drink life's gall.

Feast, and your halls are crowded;

Fast, and the world goes by.

Succeed and give, and it helps you live,

But no man can help you die.

There is room in the halls of pleasure

For a long and lordly train:

But one by one we must all file on

Through the narrow aisles of pain.

E. Nesbit (1858-1924)

Edith Nesbit defied Victorian convention by living in a ménage à trois *in south London, but despite her unusual private life she produced many charming children's stories (most famously* The Railway Children*). The down-to-earth tone of her poetry belies its thoughtful message.*

The Confession

I haven't always acted good:

I've taken things not meant for me;

Not other people's drink and food,

But things they never seemed to see.

I haven't done the way I ought

If all they say in church is true,

But all I've had I've fairly bought,

And paid for pretty heavy too.

SPIRITUAL POETRY

For days and weeks are very long
If you get nothing new and bright,
And if you never do no wrong
Somehow you never do no right.
The chap that daresent go a yard
For fear the path should lead astray
May be a saint – though that seems hard,
But he's no traveller, any way.

Some things I can't be sorry for,
The things that silly people hate;
But some I did I do deplore,
I knew, inside, they wasn't straight.
And when my last account is filed,
And stuck-up angels stop their song,

I'll ask God's pardon like a child
For what I really knew was wrong.

If you've a child, you'd rather see
A bit of temper, off and on,
A greedy grab, a silly spree
And then a brave thing said or done
Than hear your boy whine all day long
About the things he mustn't do:
Just doing nothing, right or wrong:
And God may feel the same as you.

For God's our Father, so they say,
He made His laws and He made me;
He'll understand about the way
Me and His laws could not agree.
He might say, 'You're worth more, My son,
Than all My laws since law began.
Take good with bad – here's something done
And I'm your God, and you're My man.'

AFTER DEATH

If we must part, this parting is the best:
How would you bear to lay
Your head on some warm pillow far away –
Your head, so used to lying on my breast?

134

But now your pillow is cold;

Your hands have flowers, and not my hands, to hold;

Upon our bed the worn bride-linen lies.

I have put the death-money upon your eyes,

So that you should not wake up in the night.

I have bound your face with white;

I have washed you, yes, with water and not with tears –

Those arms wherein I have slept so many years,

Those feet that hastened when they came to me,

And all your body that belonged to me.

I have smoothed your dear dull hair,

And there is nothing left to say for you

And nothing left to fear or pray for you;

And I have got the rest of life to bear:

Thank God it is you, not I, who are lying there.

If I had died

And you had stood beside

This still white bed

Where the white, scented, horrible flowers are spread –

I know the thing it is,

And I thank God that He has spared you this.

If one must bear it, thank God it was I

Who had to live and bear to see you die,

Who have to live, and bear to see you dead.

You will have nothing of it all to bear:

You will not even know that in your bed

You lie alone. You will not miss my head

Beside you on the pillow: you will rest

So soft in the grave you will not miss my breast.

But I – but I – Your pillow and your place –

And only the darkness laid against my face,
And only my anguish pressed against my side
Thank God, thank God, that it was you who died!

THE THINGS THAT MATTER

Now that I've nearly done my days,
And grown too stiff to sweep or sew,
I sit and think, till I'm amaze,
About what lots of things I know:
Things as I've found out one by one
And when I'm fast down in the day,
My knowing things and how they're done
Will all be lost and thrown away.

There's things, I know, as won't be lost,
Things as folks write and talk about:
The way to keep your roots from frost,
And how to get your ink spots out.
What medicine's good for sores and sprains,
What way to salt your butter down,
What charms will cure your different pains,
And what will bright your faded gown.
But more important things than these,
They can't be written in a book:
How fast to boil your greens and peas,
And how good bacon ought to look;
The feel of real good wearing stuff,
The kind of apple as will keep,

The look of bread that's rose enough,
And how to get a child asleep.

Whether the jam is fit to pot,
Whether the milk is going to turn,
Whether a hen will lay or not,
Is things as some folks never learn.
I know the weather by the sky,
I know what herbs grow in what lane;
And if sick men are going to die,
Or if they'll get about again.

Young wives come in, a-smiling, grave,
With secrets that they itch to tell:
I know what sort of times they'll have,
And if they'll have a boy or gell.
And if a lad is ill to bind,
Or some young maid is hard to lead,
I know when you should speak 'em kind,
And when it's scolding as they need.

I used to know where birds ud set,
And likely spots for trout or hare,
And God may want me to forget
The way to set a line or snare;
But not the way to truss a chick,
To fry a fish, or baste a roast,
Nor how to tell, when folks are sick
What kind of herb will ease them most!

Forgetting seems such silly waste!

I know so many little things,

And now the Angels will make haste

To dust it all away with wings!

O God, you made me like to know,

You kept the things straight in my head,

Please God, if you can make it so,

Let me know something when I'm dead.

RABINDRANATH TAGORE (1861-1941)

This Indian poet and philosopher was born in Calcutta and studied in England. He wrote prolifically: novels, plays and poetry and it is the latter which has survived the test of time and exercised a lasting influence on many writers throughout the world. In 1901 Tagore founded Santiniketan, a communal school which became a university, in which he attempted to combine the best of Eastern and Western thought and methods of education. He was awarded the Nobel Prize for Literature in 1913.

LAST POEMS (EXTRACT)

Now has come Man Supreme

Man after God's own heart!

The world is a-tremble with wonder

And the grass quivers.

In heaven resounds the conch,

On earth plays the drum of Victory –

The sacred moment has come

That brings the Great Birth!
The gates guarding the moonless night have fallen,
The hill of sunrise rings with the call 'Fear not'
And ushers in the dawn of a new life!
The heavens thunder the song of Victory:
'Man has come!'

ON THE SICK-BED (EXTRACT)

At noon – half awake, half asleep –
I saw as in a dream
The outer shell of my being drop off.
In the stream of the Unknown
Floated away all the gatherings of the miser –
His name, his deeds, his honour, his dishonour,
Remembrance of shame
That bore the seal of passing sweetness!
All these I cannot call back.
The Self that is beyond self, asks:
For what do I sigh most?
It is not for the past spent in joy and suffering,
But for the future, ever unattainable –
In whose heart, Hope
Like the seed in the womb of earth
Dreams through the night
For the light that is not yet come.

❧

SPIRITUAL POETRY

AMY LEVY (1861-1889)

Amy Levy led a brief and unhappy life that ended in suicide. In addition to poetry, she wrote a highly acclaimed novel, Reuben Sachs, *that dealt with the conflict between Jews and Christians in nineteenth-century English society. The small quantity of work she has left make it a source of regret that she did not live to write more.*

IN THE NOWER

Deep in the grass outstretched I lie,
Motionless on the hill;
Above me is a cloudless sky,
Around me all is still:

There is no breath, no sound, no stir,
The drowsy peace to break;
I close my tired eyes – it were
So simple not to wake.

SUSAN LANGSTAFF MITCHELL (1866-1926)

Susan Mitchell was a disciple of the mystical Irish poet 'A. E.' and a friend of the Yeats family. In addition to her most famous work, quoted here, she wrote poems, essays and drama notes for the magazine The Irish Homestead, *of which she was assistant editor.*

The Living Chalice

The Mother sent me on the holy quest,
Timid and proud and curiously dressed
In vestures by her hand wrought wondrously;
An eager burning heart she gave to me.
The Bridegroom's Feast was set and I drew nigh –
Master of Life, Thy Cup has passed me by.

Before new-dressed I from the Mother came,
In dreams I saw the wondrous Cup of Flame.
Ah, Divine Chalice, how my heart drank deep,
Waking I sought the Love I knew asleep.
The Feast of Life was set and I drew nigh –
Master of Life, Thy Cup has passed me by.

Eye of the Soul, awake, awake and see
Growing with the Ruby Radiant Tree,
Sharp pain hath wrung the clusters of my vine;
My heart is rose-red with its brimmèd wine.
Thou hast new-set the Feast and I draw nigh –
Master of Life, take me, Thy Cup am I.

Robert Frost (1874-1963)

One of America's most popular poets, nicknamed 'the voice of New England', Frost has been described as taking up the mantle of Wordsworth and Emerson in his attitude to nature and the divine. He spent the years 1912-1915 in England, where he met Rupert

Brooke and Edward Thomas, and published the collections that established his
international reputation. Much of his poetry has a deceptive air of naïveté, but – as in
this poem – there is often an underlying sense of trouble.

CARPE DIEM

Age saw two quiet children
Go loving by at twilight,
He knew not whether homeward,
Or outward from the village,
Or (chimes were ringing) churchward.
He waited (they were strangers)
Till they were out of hearing
To bid them both be happy.
'Be happy, happy, happy
And seize the day of pleasure.'
The age-long theme is Age's.
'Twas Age imposed on poems
Their gather-roses burden
To warn against the danger
That overtaken lovers
From being overflooded
With happiness should have it
And yet not know they have it.
But bid life seize the present?
It lives less in the present
Than in the future always,
And less in both together

Than in the past. The present
Is too much for the sense,
Too crowding, too confusing –
Too present to imagine.

STEVIE SMITH (1902-1971)

Stevie Smith spent most her adult life in north London, where she lived with an aunt.
She was fascinated by death, calling it 'the most exciting thing'. She also claimed not to
be able to make up her mind whether God was 'good, impotent or unkind'.

SCORPION

'This night shall thy soul be required of thee'
My soul is never required of *me*
It always has to be somebody else, of course
Will my soul be required of me tonight, perhaps?

(I often wonder what it will be like
To have one's soul required of one
But all I can think of is the Out-Patients' Department –
'Are you Mrs Briggs, dear?'
'No, I am Scorpion.')

I should like my soul to be required of me, so as
To waft over grass till it comes to the blue sea
I am very fond of grass, I always have been, but there must
Be no cow, person or house to be seen.

145

Sea and *grass* must be quite empty
Other souls can find somewhere *else.*

O Lord God please come
And require the soul of thy Scorpion

Scorpion so wishes to be gone.

LOUIS MACNEICE (1907-1963)

*The Belfast-born MacNeice spent most of his adult life in England, where he worked for
many years for the BBC and earned a reputation as a writer of superb radio plays. A
friend of W. H. Auden and Stephen Spender, whom he had met when they were all
students at Oxford, he formed part of an influential circle of left-wing poets in the 1930s.
His poetry is remarkable for its use of simple, colloquial language to express a broad
range of philosophical ideas.*

PRAYER BEFORE BIRTH

I am not yet born: O hear me,
Let not the bloodsucking bat or the rat or the stoat or the club-footed ghoul
come near me.

I am not yet born, console me.
I fear that the human race may with tall walls wall me,
with strong drugs dope me, with wise lies lure me,
on black racks rack me, in blood-baths roll me.

SPIRITUAL POETRY

I am not yet born; provide me
With water to dandle me, grass to grow for me, trees to talk to me, sky to sing to
me, birds and a white light in the back of my mind to guide me.

I am not yet born; forgive me
For the sins that in me the world shall commit, my words when they speak me,
my thoughts when they think me, my treason engendered by traitors beyond me,
my life when they murder by means of my hands, my death when they live me.

I am not yet born; rehearse me
In the parts I must play and the cues I must take when old men lecture me,
bureaucrats hector me, mountains frown at me, lovers laugh at me, the white
waves call me to folly and the desert calls me to doom and the beggar refuses
my gift and my children curse me.

I am not yet born; O hear me

Let not the man who is beast or who thinks he is God come near me.

I am not yet born; O fill me

With strength against those who would freeze my humanity, would dragoon me

into a lethal automaton, would make me a cog in a machine, a thing with one

face, a thing, and against all those who would dissipate my entirety, would blow

me like thistledown hither and thither or hither and thither like a water held in

the hands would spill me.

Let them not make me a stone and let them not spill me.

Otherwise kill me.

R. S. THOMAS (1913-2000)

An ordained minister of the Church of Wales, Ronald Stuart Thomas spent most of his
life in his native country, working in small rural communities. His poetry is centred on
Welsh life, Welsh history and a love of nature.

KNEELING

Moments of great calm,

Kneeling before an altar

Of wood in a stone church

In summer, waiting for the God

To speak; the air of a staircase

For silence; the sun's light

Ringing me, as though I acted

A great role. And the audiences
Still; all that close throng
Of spirits waiting, as I,
For the message.
Prompt me, God;
But not yet. When I speak,
Though it be you who speak
Through me, something is lost.
The meaning is in the waiting.

CHARLES CAUSLEY (1917–)

The effects of the First World War dominated Charles Causley's childhood for, although he was too young to remember it, his father returned from active service suffering from shellshock and never really recovered. The young Causley then spent six years in the Royal Navy during the Second World War, an event which influenced much of his later writing. After the war he became a teacher in his native Cornwall and wrote both verse and stories for children. This late poem shows a characteristic simplicity of style.

EDEN ROCK

They are waiting for me somewhere beyond Eden Rock:
My father, twenty-five, in the same suit
Of Genuine Irish Tweed, his terrier Jack
Still two years old and trembling at his feet.

My mother, twenty-three, in a sprigged dress
Drawn at the waist, ribbon in her straw hat,

Has spread the stiff white cloth over the grass.
Her hair, the colour of wheat, takes on the light.

She pours tea from a Thermos, the milk straight
From an old H. P. sauce bottle, a screw
Of paper for a cork; slowly sets out
The same three plates, the tin cups painted blue.

The sky whitens as if lit by three suns.
My mother shades her eyes and looks my way
Over the drifted stream. My father spins
A stone along the water. Leisurely,
They beckon to me from the other bank.
I hear them call, 'See where the stream-path is!
Crossing is not as hard as you might think.'

I had not thought that it would be like this.

PAUL CELAN (1920-1970)

Paul Celan was born in a small Rumanian town in what is now the Ukraine. The Germans invaded in 1941 and forced his family, along with other Jews, into a ghetto. Both his parents subsequently died in a concentration camp. The young Celan survived several years in a labour camp, but the experience understandably darkened his view of life. After the war he studied in Bucharest and worked as a translator of Russian literature into Rumanian. He then spent a brief period in Vienna, where his first poems were published, before settling in Paris. There he met the famous artists and writers of the time and produced dark, haunting poems about the difficulties of life and relationships. This one was translated by Michael Hamburger.

TENEBRAE

We are near, Lord,
near and at hand.
Handled already, Lord,
clawed and clawing as though
the body of each of us were
your body, Lord.

Pray, Lord,
pray to us,
we are near.

Wind-awry we went there,
went there to bend
over hollow and ditch.

To be watered we went there, Lord.

It was blood, it was
what you shed, Lord.
It gleamed.

It cast your image into our eyes, Lord.
Our eyes and our mouths are so open and empty, Lord.
We have drunk, Lord.
The blood and the image that was in the blood, Lord.

Pray, Lord.
We are near.

JOHN AGARD (1949–)

Born in Guyana, John Agard moved to Britain in 1977 where he worked at the Commonwealth Institute and visited over two thousand schools, discussing his life in the Caribbean and giving readings and workshops. He later became Poet in Residence at the BBC and played a key role in their Windrush season, which marked the fiftieth anniversary of the first major wave of West Indian poetry. He has published a number of collections of poems both for adults and for children.

RAINBOW

When you see
de rainbow
you know
God know
what he doing –
one big smile
across the sky –
I tell you
God got style
the man got style

When you see
raincloud pass
and de rainbow
make a show
I tell you
is God doing
limbo

the man doing

limbo

But sometimes

you know

when I see

de rainbow

so full of glow

& curving

like she bearing child

I does want to know

if God

ain't a woman

If that is so

the woman got style

man she got style

INDEX OF FIRST LINES

Oh when I come to die 83
Once more they ventured from the dust to raise 31

Poor soul, the centre of my sinful earth 51

Since Nature's works be good, and death doth serve 50
So humble things Thou hast borne for us, O God 130
Speed forth, O Soul! upon thy star-strewn path 127

The moon now rises to her absolute rule 96
The Mother sent me on the holy quest 143
The spacous firmament on high 68
The sun, the moon, the stars, the seas, the hills and the plains 95
Then was not non-existent nor existent 12
'There is no God,' the wicked saith 104
They are waiting for me somewhere beyond Eden Rock 149
'This night shall thy soul be required of thee' 145
Thou dear and mystic semblance 81
Though I am weak and tired now 19
Through that pure Virgin-shrine 65
Throw away Thy rod 56
To see a world in a grain of sand 74

Vital spark of heav'nly flame! 70

We are near, Lord 151
What a restful life is his 44
What household thoughts around thee, as their shrine 80
What is our life? A play of passion 50
When carrying on your head your perplexed bodily soul 17
When I consider how my light is spent 58
When I have fears that I may cease to be 78
When upon revellers the stained dawn breaks 110
When you see de rainbow 152
Wherever my eyes turn 38
Who would true valour see 67
With this ambiguous earth 128

Yes! Thou art Parabrahm! The High Abode! 19
You say, 'Where goest thou?' I cannot tell 89